Value Realized

The Executive Guide to Enterprise Execution and Value Realization

By Kevin Morris

Published by
Antioch Value Assurance
Spring, Texas

First Edition

Printed in the United States of America

ISBN (Paperback): 979-8-9966078-0-8
ISBN (Kindle eBook): 979-8-9966078-1-5

Cover design by Antioch Value Assurance
Interior design by Kevin Morris

For information regarding speaking engagements, consulting services, or corporate training:

Antioch Value Assurance
kevin.morris@antiochvalueassurance.com
www.antiochvalueassurance.com

Table of Contents

Preface

For most of my career, I have worked in environments where the stakes were high, the timelines were compressed, and the consequences of failure were measured not in theory, but in dollars, disrupted operations, delayed synergies, missed opportunities, and unrealized value.

Over the past thirty years, I have had the privilege of leading and supporting mergers, acquisitions, divestitures, separations, technology transformations, and enterprise change initiatives across a wide range of organizations. Some delivered extraordinary results. Others struggled despite strong strategies, talented people, and significant investments.

Over time, one observation became increasingly difficult to ignore.

Organizations rarely fail because they lack strategy.

They fail because they struggle to execute.

The business case may be compelling. The financial analysis may be sound. The transaction rationale may be clear. Yet somewhere between executive approval and realized benefits, value begins to erode. Decisions slow. Priorities compete. Accountability becomes unclear. Risks emerge. Momentum fades. Expected outcomes become delayed or disappear entirely.

This book was written to explore that gap.

Value Realized is not a book about a particular industry, consulting methodology, or proprietary solution. It is a book about execution and the challenge organizations face in converting intentions into outcomes. While many of the examples draw from mergers, acquisitions, and large-scale transformations, the principles discussed here apply equally to strategic initiatives, operational improvements, technology programs, and enterprise change efforts of every kind.

Throughout my career, I have worked alongside exceptional leaders, project managers, integration teams, technical specialists, and business professionals. The ideas presented in these pages are shaped not only by my own experiences, but also by countless lessons learned from colleagues, mentors, sponsors, and teams who faced difficult challenges and worked tirelessly to deliver results.

My hope is that this book contributes to a larger conversation about execution.

Organizations invest tremendous effort developing strategy, evaluating opportunities, and designing future-state visions. Yet comparatively little attention is given to the organizational capacity required to execute those decisions successfully. We often ask whether an initiative is strategically sound or financially justified, but we ask less frequently whether the organization possesses the alignment, governance, leadership, and execution capability necessary to realize the intended value.

The concepts presented in this book are intended to encourage discussion, challenge assumptions, and provide practical ideas that leaders can apply within their own organizations. Readers may adopt some of these approaches, adapt others, or develop entirely different methods. The objective is not to prescribe a single answer, but to advance the discipline of enterprise execution and value realization.

If this book helps a leader ask better questions, improve governance, strengthen accountability, reduce value leakage, or better support the people responsible for execution, then it will have achieved its purpose.

The future success of organizations will depend less on their ability to create strategy and increasingly on their ability to execute it.

Because in the end, value is not created when decisions are made.

Value is realized when execution delivers the intended outcome.

— Kevin Morris

Introduction

Most organizations do not fail because they lack strategy.

They fail because they struggle to execute.

Every year, companies invest billions of dollars pursuing acquisitions, implementing new technologies, restructuring operations, launching transformations, and pursuing strategic initiatives intended to create enterprise value. Leadership teams spend months developing business cases, conducting due diligence, building financial models, and securing approvals. Consultants develop recommendations. Program teams create plans. Executive presentations promise significant benefits.

Yet somewhere between intention and outcome, value begins to disappear.

Synergies fail to materialize. Decisions are delayed. Risks emerge unexpectedly. Technology creates friction. Organizations become overwhelmed by competing priorities. Teams lose momentum. Leadership attention shifts elsewhere. The very initiatives designed to create value begin to consume it.

This phenomenon is not limited to mergers and acquisitions.

The same challenges exist in major capital projects, digital transformations, organizational redesigns, technology implementations, separation programs, and enterprise-wide initiatives. Organizations repeatedly discover that success depends less upon strategy itself and more upon the ability to execute consistently, lead effectively, and sustain focus over time.

After more than thirty years leading mergers, acquisitions, divestitures, technology transformations, and enterprise programs around the world, I have reached a simple conclusion:

Value is not created through intention. Value is realized through execution.

Throughout my career, I have worked alongside executive leadership teams, integration organizations, technology groups, business functions, and operational leaders facing extraordinary challenges. Some organizations consistently achieved their objectives. Others struggled despite having talented people, strong strategies, and significant resources.

The difference was rarely intelligence.

The difference was execution.

The organizations that succeeded understood that value realization requires multiple disciplines working together. Strategy alone is insufficient. Governance alone is insufficient. Technology alone is insufficient. Leadership alone is insufficient.

Enterprise value realization demands an integrated system.

That realization became the foundation of the AVA Enterprise Value Realization System.

The AVA system is built upon five interconnected pillars that collectively determine whether value is ultimately realized.

AVA Assess™ helps organizations understand opportunity, readiness, complexity, risk, and the conditions necessary for success before execution begins.

AVA Execute™ provides the structure, governance, planning, accountability, and operational discipline required to deliver results.

AVA Lead™ focuses on leadership alignment, communication, organizational readiness, and the human dimensions of transformation.

AVA Tech™ ensures that technology enables the business through effective architecture, integration, cybersecurity, data management, and digital capabilities.

AVA Exit™ protects long-term value through transition readiness, operational sustainability, dependency retirement, and successful separation or handover.

Supporting these pillars are two enterprise-wide capabilities.

AVA Intelligence™ represents the growing importance of analytics, artificial intelligence, predictive insights, and decision support. The future of value realization will increasingly depend upon organizations that can transform information into foresight and foresight into action.

AVA Assure™ provides continuous value assurance across the entire system. Independent reviews, performance validation, benefits realization, risk monitoring, and executive oversight help organizations maintain confidence that value remains achievable and measurable.

Together, these capabilities create a comprehensive approach to enterprise value realization.

But this book is not simply about frameworks.

It is about leadership.

It is about accountability.

It is about helping organizations deliver on their promises.

It is about protecting the investments that shareholders, employees, customers, and communities depend upon.

Perhaps most importantly, it is about passing knowledge forward.

Throughout my career, I have been fortunate to learn from experienced leaders who shared their knowledge, their mistakes, and their wisdom. Many of the lessons contained in these pages were earned through difficult experiences, challenging decisions, and moments when success was far from certain.

As our industries continue to evolve, many of those experiences risk being lost as experienced professionals retire and organizations become increasingly focused on short-term results. One of the motivations behind this book is to preserve those lessons for the next generation of leaders who will inherit increasingly complex transformations and ever-growing expectations.

The future leaders of our organizations must understand not only how to build plans, but how to lead people. They must understand not only how to manage technology, but how to create confidence. They must understand not only how to execute projects, but how to realize value.

This book is written for executives, transformation leaders, integration teams, program managers, technology leaders, private equity professionals, and anyone responsible for delivering meaningful business outcomes.

Some readers may be leading an acquisition.

Others may be managing a separation.

Some may be responsible for a technology transformation.

Others may simply want to become better leaders.

Regardless of the challenge, the principles remain the same.

Assess the opportunity.

Execute with discipline.

Lead people through change.

Enable value through technology.

Prepare for sustainable transition.

Apply intelligence.

Provide assurance.

Protect value.

Realize results.

The chapters that follow explore these principles in detail while providing practical guidance, real-world examples, and lessons learned from decades of experience.

Because at the end of every transaction, every transformation, every integration, and every strategic initiative, one question ultimately remains:

Did we realize the value we intended to create?

That is the question this book seeks to answer.

PART I - THE EXECUTION PROBLEM

Organizations have never had more access to information, technology, capital, and expertise than they do today. Strategic plans are carefully developed. Transactions are thoroughly analyzed. Business cases are extensively modeled. Executive teams establish ambitious objectives and organizations invest enormous resources pursuing growth, transformation, and improvement. Yet despite these efforts, many organizations consistently struggle to realize the value they expected.

The problem is rarely the strategy itself. Most organizations understand what they are trying to accomplish. The challenge begins when strategy must become execution. Competing priorities emerge, resources become constrained, decisions slow, technology introduces complexity, and organizational capacity becomes stretched. The gap between expected value and realized value begins to widen, often gradually and sometimes invisibly.

The chapters in this section examine the realities that prevent organizations from achieving the outcomes they seek. They explore the execution crisis affecting modern organizations, the silent erosion of value through value leakage, the growing challenge of organizational capacity, and the limitations of strategy alone. Understanding these challenges is essential because organizations cannot solve a problem, they do not fully recognize.

Before value can be realized, leaders must first understand why value is so often lost. Because the greatest obstacle facing many organizations today is not a lack of vision, strategy, or ambition.

It is the challenge of execution.

Chapter 1 - The M&A Execution Crisis

Every year, organizations around the world announce mergers, acquisitions, divestitures, and strategic transactions worth trillions of dollars. Executive teams describe transformative opportunities, expanded markets, operational efficiencies, technology advantages, and significant financial benefits. Investors anticipate increased shareholder value. Employees are promised new opportunities. Customers expect improved capabilities and services.

The deal is announced.

The press release is issued.

The financial markets react.

And then the real work begins.

Despite the experience of executive teams, the sophistication of financial advisors, and the rigor of due diligence efforts, many transactions fail to deliver the value that justified the investment. Expected synergies fall short. Integration activities take longer than planned. Costs exceed forecasts. Technology issues emerge. Key employees leave. Customers become frustrated. Operational performance suffers. In some cases, organizations spend years attempting to recover from decisions made during the earliest stages of execution.

The challenge facing modern mergers and acquisitions is not a lack of intelligence, financial analysis, or strategic planning. The challenge is execution.

For decades, studies have consistently suggested that a significant percentage of mergers and acquisitions fail to achieve their anticipated objectives. While individual studies differ in methodology and measurement, the overall conclusion remains remarkably consistent. Many transactions underperform expectations, and a substantial portion of anticipated value is never realized.

The reasons are rarely found within the financial model.

They are found within the execution.

Organizations frequently devote months evaluating acquisition targets, building valuation models, conducting due diligence, and negotiating transaction terms. Yet comparatively little attention is given to the organization's actual ability to execute the change that follows. Questions surrounding organizational readiness, leadership capacity, decision making, technology complexity, and operational dependencies often receive far less attention than purchase price adjustments or synergy estimates.

The transaction closes.

The integration begins.

And organizations discover that the greatest risks were not identified during due diligence.

They emerge afterward.

Throughout my career leading integrations, separations, and enterprise transformations, I have observed this pattern repeatedly. The issues that ultimately threaten value are often predictable. Executive decisions are delayed. Functional leaders lack available capacity. Governance becomes inconsistent. Technology dependencies are underestimated. Risks accumulate faster than they are addressed. Teams become overwhelmed by competing priorities. Benefits become difficult to measure and even more difficult to sustain.

These problems rarely appear in the original deal model.

Yet they determine whether the transaction succeeds.

The Hidden Complexity of Execution

Modern organizations have become highly optimized for operational efficiency. Functions operate with fewer resources. Subject matter experts support multiple initiatives simultaneously. Teams have limited capacity to absorb large-scale change while maintaining daily operations. Technology environments have become increasingly interconnected. Regulatory requirements continue to expand. Global organizations must coordinate activities across multiple regions, time zones, and business cultures.

As organizations have become more efficient, they have often become less capable of absorbing significant change.

Mergers and acquisitions place enormous demands upon an organization. Leaders must continue operating the existing business while simultaneously integrating systems, restructuring organizations, managing employees, communicating with customers, addressing regulatory requirements, and delivering expected financial results.

This challenge is frequently underestimated.

Transactions do not fail because organizations lack intelligent people.

They fail because organizations lack sufficient execution capacity.

The Cost of Value Leakage

Value leakage occurs whenever expected benefits fail to materialize because of execution challenges. Synergies may be delayed. Revenue opportunities may be lost. Operating costs may increase. Customers may leave. Employees may become disengaged. Technology projects may experience delays. Regulatory issues may emerge. Operational disruptions may occur.

These losses often occur gradually.

A delayed decision here.

A missed dependency there.

An unresolved issue.

An unavailable resource.

A technology risk that receives insufficient attention.

Individually, these events may appear insignificant. Collectively, they can substantially reduce the value a transaction was expected to deliver.

One of the most important lessons learned from decades of transaction experience is that value rarely disappears all at once.

Value leaks.

It leaks through poor decisions, delayed actions, inadequate governance, insufficient resources, unclear accountability, and ineffective execution.

By the time financial results reveal the problem, much of the damage has already occurred.

Why Traditional Approaches Fall Short

Traditional transaction approaches often emphasize the front end of the deal. Significant resources are dedicated to strategy, valuation, due diligence, negotiations, and closing activities. While these activities are essential, they represent only the beginning of value creation.

Execution receives less attention because it is difficult.

Execution cannot be completed in a conference room.

It cannot be delegated entirely to consultants.

It cannot be solved solely through financial analysis.

Execution requires leadership.

It requires governance.

It requires organizational capacity.

It requires disciplined decision making.

It requires continuous attention to risk, dependencies, and outcomes.

Perhaps most importantly, it requires organizations to recognize that the transaction itself is not the objective.

The objective is realizing value.

The Emerging Execution Gap

Today, organizations face what can best be described as an execution gap.

The pace of change continues to accelerate. Transactions have become more complex. Technology environments have expanded. Business expectations continue to increase. Yet organizational capacity has often remained unchanged or declined.

Leaders ask the same teams to support multiple initiatives simultaneously.

Employees maintain their operational responsibilities while participating in major transformations.

Critical subject matter experts become bottlenecks.

Decision making slows.

Priorities compete.

Execution suffers.

This gap between strategic ambition and execution capability represents one of the most significant challenges facing modern enterprises.

Organizations no longer compete solely on strategy.

They compete on execution.

A New Way of Thinking

The future of successful mergers, acquisitions, and transformations will belong to organizations that treat execution as a strategic capability rather than a project management activity.

These organizations understand that value must be intentionally protected, measured, and realized. They recognize that leadership, governance, technology, organizational readiness, and benefits realization are equally important. They understand that execution is not a temporary phase of the transaction lifecycle but a core enterprise capability.

This realization eventually led to the development of the Enterprise Value Realization philosophy and the AVA Enterprise Value Realization System. However, before discussing frameworks, methodologies, or solutions, it is necessary to understand the problem itself.

The M&A industry does not suffer from a strategy crisis.

It suffers from an execution crisis.

Until organizations address that reality, the gap between expected value and realized value will continue to grow.

And the value that justified the transaction in the first place will continue to disappear long after the deal has closed.

Chapter 2 - Value Leakage: The Silent Enterprise Killer

The most dangerous threats to a transaction are rarely the ones discussed in the boardroom.

Organizations spend months evaluating financial risks, legal exposures, regulatory concerns, market conditions, and competitive threats. Extensive due diligence is conducted. Advisors produce detailed analyses. Financial models are scrutinized. Executives debate valuation assumptions and strategic alternatives.

Yet the greatest threat to enterprise value often receives far less attention.

Value leakage.

Value leakage is the gradual loss of anticipated benefits, synergies, efficiencies, and strategic outcomes that occurs during execution. It does not usually result from a single catastrophic event. Instead, it develops through hundreds of small decisions, unresolved issues, delayed actions, competing priorities, and overlooked risks that accumulate over time.

By the time organizations recognize the problem, much of the value has already disappeared.

This is what makes value leakage so dangerous.

It is often invisible.

It rarely appears on financial statements in real time.

It is difficult to measure.

And it frequently becomes accepted as part of the normal challenges associated with mergers, acquisitions, separations, and enterprise transformations.

In reality, value leakage is neither unavoidable nor acceptable.

It is one of the most important leadership challenges facing modern organizations.

Value Does Not Disappear Overnight

When transactions underperform, executives often search for a single explanation.

Perhaps the acquisition price was too high.

Perhaps market conditions changed.

Perhaps the business environment deteriorated.

Perhaps assumptions proved incorrect.

While these factors certainly influence outcomes, the majority of lost value typically occurs through a series of relatively small events.

A decision delayed by three weeks.

A technology dependency that was not identified.

A resource assigned to competing priorities.

An unresolved issue that affects multiple workstreams.

A synergy initiative that loses executive sponsorship.

A customer communication that occurs too late.

A leadership vacancy.

An underestimated transition activity.

Individually, these events may appear insignificant. Collectively, they can substantially reduce the value expected from the transaction.

Value rarely disappears all at once.

It leaks.

The cumulative impact of these small failures often becomes visible only after months have passed and opportunities can no longer be recovered.

The Sources of Value Leakage

Value leakage occurs in multiple forms. Some are operational. Others are organizational. Many are behavioral. Understanding these sources is the first step toward preventing them.

Leadership Leakage

Leadership teams often become heavily involved during transaction approval and closing activities. Once the transaction closes, attention shifts toward other priorities.

Without visible executive sponsorship, priorities become unclear. Decisions slow. Accountability weakens. Teams lose direction.

Leadership attention is one of the most important value protection mechanisms an organization possesses.

When leadership engagement declines, value leakage accelerates.

Decision Leakage

Transactions require thousands of decisions.

Operating models.

Technology platforms.

Organizational structures.

Processes.

Policies.

Resource allocations.

The longer decisions remain unresolved, the greater the impact on execution.

Teams wait.

Dependencies accumulate.

Schedules slip.

Risks increase.

Decision velocity often becomes one of the strongest predictors of execution success.

Slow decisions create fast problems.

Capacity Leakage

Modern organizations operate with lean staffing models and limited excess capacity. Subject matter experts often support daily operations while simultaneously participating in integration or transformation activities.

Employees become overloaded.

Meetings increase.

Priorities compete.

Critical tasks are delayed.

Execution suffers.

Many organizations underestimate the capacity required to absorb change.

The issue is not a lack of commitment.

It is a lack of available bandwidth.

Technology Leakage

Technology is frequently one of the largest contributors to value loss.

Data migration delays.

Cybersecurity concerns.

ERP dependencies.

Application rationalization challenges.

Infrastructure issues.

Integration complexities.

Technology problems can affect every workstream simultaneously. When technology issues emerge, operational performance often suffers, decision making slows, and confidence declines.

Technology no longer supports transactions.

It enables or constrains them.

Governance Leakage

Poor governance creates uncertainty.

Unclear decision rights.

Conflicting priorities.

Inconsistent reporting.

Delayed escalations.

Undefined accountability.

Without effective governance, organizations struggle to coordinate activities across functions and leadership levels.

Issues remain unresolved.

Risks remain unmanaged.

Value begins to disappear.

Benefits Leakage

Perhaps the most overlooked form of value leakage occurs after implementation activities have concluded.

The transaction closes.

The systems go live.

The transition ends.

The teams disband.

But the expected benefits never materialize.

Cost reductions fail to occur.

Revenue synergies are delayed.

Operational improvements are not measured.

Accountability disappears.

Organizations frequently declare success before value has actually been realized.

Benefits that are not measured are rarely achieved.

The Hidden Cost of Delay

Time itself can become a source of value leakage.

Delayed integrations postpone synergies.

Extended TSAs increase costs.

Deferred decisions reduce momentum.

Prolonged uncertainty affects employees and customers.

Execution speed matters because value has a time component.

Benefits realized six months late often have significantly lower value than benefits achieved on schedule.

Organizations frequently focus on cost overruns while overlooking the financial impact of delayed outcomes.

Delay is not neutral.

Delay destroys value.

Why Organizations Miss the Warning Signs

Value leakage is difficult to identify because most organizations measure activities rather than outcomes.

Project plans appear green.

Status reports show progress.

Milestones are completed.

Meetings occur.

Deliverables are produced.

Yet value continues to disappear.

Traditional reporting often measures whether tasks have been completed rather than whether value is being protected.

Organizations need leading indicators.

Decision cycle times.

Resource availability.

Risk trends.

Issue aging.

Dependency health.

Benefits performance.

Executive engagement.

Without these indicators, leadership teams often discover value erosion only after financial results begin to decline.

By then, recovery becomes significantly more difficult.

The Importance of Value Assurance

The recognition that value leakage could be measured, monitored, and reduced led to an important realization.

Organizations require mechanisms that continuously evaluate whether value is being protected throughout execution.

Traditional project management measures activity.

Financial reporting measures results.

Neither consistently measures value realization.

This gap creates the need for continuous value assurance.

Value assurance focuses on identifying emerging risks, monitoring leading indicators, validating benefits, and ensuring accountability for outcomes. It recognizes that protecting value requires continuous attention throughout the lifecycle of a transaction or transformation.

Organizations that successfully manage value leakage do not eliminate risk.

They identify risk earlier.

They make decisions faster.

They maintain accountability.

They measure outcomes.

They intervene before problems become irreversible.

A Leadership Responsibility

Value leakage is often viewed as an operational issue.

In reality, it is a leadership issue.

Leaders establish priorities.

Leaders allocate resources.

Leaders make decisions.

Leaders establish accountability.

Leaders determine whether benefits are measured and realized.

The organizations that consistently deliver value are not necessarily those with the best financial models, the most sophisticated strategies, or the largest integration teams.

They are the organizations that recognize value as something that must be actively protected.

They understand that value does not automatically appear because a transaction closes.

Value must be managed.

Value must be measured.

Value must be assured.

Because value lost during execution is rarely recovered later.

And what organizations fail to protect, they eventually lose.

Chapter 3 - The Capacity Problem

One of the most dangerous assumptions made during mergers, acquisitions, separations, and enterprise transformations is also one of the least discussed.

The assumption is simple:

The organization will somehow find the time.

Executives approve the transaction. Integration plans are developed. Synergies are identified. Technology projects are launched. Functional workstreams are established. Milestones are assigned.

And then leadership turns to the existing organization and asks it to deliver all of the work.

The same people.

The same teams.

The same resources.

The same operating budgets.

While continuing to run the business.

This assumption lies at the heart of what may be the most significant challenge facing modern organizations:

The capacity problem.

Organizations Have Become Lean

Over the past several decades, organizations have pursued efficiency aggressively. Layers of management have been reduced. Functional organizations have become smaller. Support functions have been streamlined. Spans of control have increased. Teams have been expected to accomplish more with fewer resources.

These changes have often improved operating efficiency.

However, they have also reduced organizational flexibility.

Most organizations today operate with little excess capacity. Employees manage full workloads. Subject matter experts support multiple responsibilities. Leaders oversee larger organizations than ever before. Critical personnel frequently become single points of failure.

Under normal operating conditions, these organizations may perform exceptionally well.

Under conditions of significant change, they often struggle.

The challenge is not operational efficiency.

The challenge is the ability to absorb change.

The Myth of Available Resources

Transaction plans frequently assume that business resources will be available when needed.

Finance leaders will support data validation.

Human resources teams will assist with organizational changes.

Information technology personnel will lead system integrations.

Operations teams will redesign processes.

Legal departments will address contract issues.

Supply chain teams will support transitions.

But these individuals already have full-time responsibilities.

They continue supporting customers.

They continue closing financial periods.

They continue maintaining systems.

They continue operating plants, facilities, and businesses.

The transaction becomes additional work.

Organizations often describe these individuals as "part-time resources."

In reality, many become full-time employees with two full-time jobs.

This situation is unsustainable.

Eventually, priorities compete.

Deadlines slip.

Decisions are delayed.

Issues remain unresolved.

Value begins to leak.

The Hidden Cost of Overload

When organizations exceed their execution capacity, the effects become visible throughout the enterprise.

Meetings increase.

Email volume expands.

Decision making slows.

Issue backlogs grow.

Project schedules slip.

Risk levels increase.

Employees experience frustration and fatigue.

High performers become overwhelmed because they are asked to solve the greatest number of problems. Subject matter experts become bottlenecks because every decision requires their involvement. Leaders spend more time reacting to issues than managing outcomes.

The organization becomes increasingly busy.

But productivity declines.

This distinction is important.

Activity does not equal progress.

Organizations can work harder while accomplishing less.

The Capacity Gap

Every major transaction creates two competing demands.

The business must continue operating successfully.

The organization must simultaneously execute significant change.

This creates what can be described as the capacity gap.

The capacity gap is the difference between the amount of change required and the organization's ability to absorb and execute that change.

As the gap widens, execution risk increases.

Decision quality declines.

Leadership attention becomes fragmented.

Teams become overwhelmed.

Benefits are delayed.

Value leakage accelerates.

Most transactions do not fail because organizations underestimate the amount of work required.

They fail because organizations overestimate their ability to absorb it.

Execution Capacity as a Strategic Asset

Organizations routinely evaluate financial capacity.

They assess debt capacity.

They evaluate investment capacity.

They measure manufacturing capacity.

They analyze production capacity.

Yet few organizations evaluate execution capacity.

Questions such as these are rarely asked:

- Do we have enough leadership bandwidth?
- Do we have sufficient subject matter expertise?
- Can the organization absorb this level of change?
- Are our critical resources already committed elsewhere?
- How many major initiatives are occurring simultaneously?
- What functions represent bottlenecks?
- What decisions require executive attention?

Execution capacity should be evaluated with the same rigor as financial performance.

Because a strategy that exceeds organizational capacity cannot be successfully executed.

The Human Side of Capacity

Capacity is not merely a resource problem.

It is also a human problem.

Employees experiencing constant change often encounter uncertainty, fatigue, and frustration. New systems must be learned. Reporting relationships change. Processes evolve. Expectations increase.

Meanwhile, daily responsibilities remain.

The cumulative effect can be significant.

Employees disengage.

Turnover increases.

Collaboration declines.

Resistance grows.

Organizations frequently interpret resistance as unwillingness to change.

In many cases, employees are not resisting change.

They are overwhelmed by it.

Recognizing this distinction is essential.

Organizations cannot simply demand additional effort indefinitely.

Capacity has limits.

Leadership Capacity

Executives and senior leaders face similar challenges.

Mergers and acquisitions require hundreds of decisions.

Operating models.

Organization structures.

Technology choices.

Investment priorities.

Risk responses.

Communication strategies.

At the same time, leaders continue managing ongoing business responsibilities.

Their calendars become saturated.

Decision queues develop.

Issues remain unresolved.

The speed of execution slows.

Leadership capacity often becomes one of the largest constraints within the organization.

Decision velocity depends upon available leadership attention.

When leadership becomes overloaded, the entire organization slows.

Building Capacity for Execution

Organizations that consistently deliver value recognize that execution capacity must be intentionally developed.

This may involve:

- Dedicated integration teams.
- Integration management offices.
- Temporary backfill resources.
- External expertise.
- Prioritization of initiatives.
- Clear decision rights.
- Executive governance.
- Resource planning.

Successful organizations do not assume capacity exists.

They create it.

They protect it.

They manage it.

Execution capacity becomes an investment rather than an assumption.

The Importance of Assessment

One of the most important lessons learned from decades of transaction experience is that organizations often evaluate the target company more thoroughly than they evaluate themselves.

Extensive due diligence may be performed on financial statements, systems, contracts, and operations.

Yet little attention is given to the acquiring organization's own readiness to execute.

Questions regarding capacity, leadership bandwidth, organizational preparedness, competing initiatives, and resource constraints often remain unanswered.

Understanding these conditions before execution begins can significantly improve outcomes.

Organizations that assess readiness and capacity early are better positioned to identify risks, allocate resources, and protect value.

Those that ignore capacity frequently discover the problem only after execution begins.

At that point, recovery becomes far more difficult.

The New Competitive Advantage

For decades, organizations competed primarily on strategy.

Today, they increasingly compete on execution.

And execution depends upon capacity.

The organizations that consistently realize value are not always those with the largest budgets, the most sophisticated financial models, or the most ambitious strategies.

They are often the organizations that understand their limitations.

They invest in their people.

They create leadership capacity.

They protect critical resources.

They assess readiness honestly.

They recognize that execution is not free.

Execution requires people.

Execution requires time.

Execution requires leadership.

Execution requires capacity.

Because no matter how compelling the strategy may be, no organization can execute beyond its ability to absorb change.

And when execution demand exceeds organizational capacity, value is often the first casualty.

Chapter 4 - Why Strategy Is Not Enough

Organizations have never invested more time, money, and intellectual energy in strategy than they do today.

Executive teams conduct strategic planning sessions. Consultants facilitate workshops. Financial models are developed. Market analyses are performed. Synergy estimates are calculated. Transformation roadmaps are created. Business cases are approved. Objectives are established.

The result is often a well-defined strategy.

Yet many organizations still fail to achieve the outcomes they expected.

This contradiction raises an important question.

If organizations possess intelligent leaders, experienced advisors, sophisticated analytics, and well-developed strategies, why do so many transformations underperform?

The answer is both simple and uncomfortable.

Strategy alone does not create value.

Execution does.

The Strategy Illusion

Strategy is essential.

Without a clear direction, organizations struggle to align priorities, allocate resources, or make effective decisions. Strategy establishes purpose. It identifies opportunities. It communicates objectives. It defines what success should look like.

But strategy itself creates no value.

A synergy target does not reduce costs.

A business case does not improve operations.

A financial model does not generate cash flow.

A transformation roadmap does not change behavior.

These documents describe expected outcomes.

They do not produce them.

Organizations often mistake planning for progress because planning feels productive. Meetings occur. Presentations are developed. Decisions are documented. Roadmaps are approved.

The organization gains confidence.

Yet little has actually changed.

Real value begins only when execution starts.

The Closing Myth

Many organizations unconsciously treat transaction closing as the finish line.

The deal is announced.

The transaction closes.

The market reacts.

The teams celebrate.

But closing is not the end.

It is the starting point.

The financial model assumes that synergies will occur.

The business case assumes operational improvements.

The acquisition thesis assumes organizational change.

The transaction merely creates the opportunity to realize value.

Whether that value is ultimately achieved depends entirely upon what happens afterward.

Some of the most difficult work occurs after the transaction closes:

- Integrating organizations.
- Migrating technology.
- Aligning leadership.
- Making decisions.
- Managing risk.
- Changing processes.
- Retaining employees.
- Supporting customers.
- Measuring benefits.

This work determines whether value is realized.

The Execution Gap

Every organization experiences some degree of separation between strategy and execution.

This can be described as the execution gap.

The execution gap exists between:

- Expected benefits and realized benefits.
- Planned outcomes and actual results.
- Strategic intent and operational performance.
- Executive expectations and organizational capacity.

The larger the gap becomes, the greater the value loss.

Many organizations devote enormous effort to determining what they should do while investing far less energy in determining how they will successfully do it.

Questions often remain unanswered.

Who owns the benefit?

Who makes decisions?

Who resolves conflicts?

Who measures progress?

Who manages risk?

Who ensures accountability?

Without answers, execution becomes inconsistent.

The strategy remains sound.

The results do not.

Complexity Changes Everything

Modern business environments have become extraordinarily complex.

Organizations operate across multiple geographies.

Technology systems are interconnected.

Regulatory requirements continue to expand.

Supply chains are global.

Organizations manage multiple transformations simultaneously.

Employees support numerous competing priorities.

These conditions make execution significantly more difficult than strategy development.

A leadership team may develop a strategic plan over several weeks.

Executing that strategy may require years of sustained effort.

It requires hundreds of decisions.

Thousands of activities.

Dozens of teams.

Numerous dependencies.

Significant leadership attention.

Execution occurs within complexity.

And complexity often defeats good intentions.

Leadership and Execution

Organizations frequently assign strategy to executives and execution to project teams.

This division creates problems.

Execution is not simply an operational responsibility.

It is a leadership responsibility.

Leaders establish priorities.

Leaders allocate resources.

Leaders make decisions.

Leaders remove obstacles.

Leaders maintain accountability.

When leadership engagement declines after strategy approval, organizations often lose momentum.

Priorities become unclear.

Decisions slow.

Risks increase.

Value begins to leak.

Successful organizations understand that leadership does not end when the strategy is approved.

Leadership becomes even more important during execution.

The Problem with Traditional Measures

Many organizations measure strategic activities rather than value outcomes.

They track:

- Milestones completed.
- Tasks finished.
- Meetings held.
- Reports produced.
- Budgets spent.

These activities provide useful information.

However, they do not answer the most important question.

Is value actually being realized?

Organizations may complete every milestone and still fail to achieve the expected benefits.

Projects may finish on schedule while value continues to decline.

Budgets may remain under control while synergies fail to materialize.

Execution success cannot be measured solely by activity.

It must be measured by outcomes.

Execution as a Strategic Capability

Some organizations consistently outperform others.

They execute faster.

They make decisions more effectively.

They adapt to change more successfully.

They realize greater value.

The difference is rarely strategy alone.

The difference is execution capability.

Execution capability includes:

- Organizational readiness.
- Leadership alignment.
- Governance.
- Accountability.

- Decision velocity.
- Resource capacity.
- Risk management.
- Technology readiness.
- Benefits realization.

These capabilities do not emerge automatically.

They must be intentionally developed.

Organizations that treat execution as a strategic capability create sustainable advantages that competitors often struggle to replicate.

The Rise of Enterprise Value Realization

The recognition that execution determines outcomes leads to an important conclusion.

Organizations require a more comprehensive approach.

One that extends beyond strategy.

One that connects leadership, governance, technology, organizational readiness, and benefits realization.

One that focuses not simply on completing projects but on realizing value.

This discipline can be described as Enterprise Value Realization.

Enterprise Value Realization recognizes that:

- Value must be intentionally protected.
- Benefits must be actively managed.
- Risks must be identified early.
- Decisions must occur quickly.
- Leadership must remain engaged.
- Technology must support execution.

- Organizations must possess sufficient capacity.
- Outcomes must be measured.

Execution becomes the bridge between strategy and value.

Without execution, strategy remains theoretical.

Without value realization, strategy remains incomplete.

Beyond Strategy

The organizations that succeed in the future will not necessarily have better strategies.

They will execute better.

They will understand their capacity.

They will identify value leakage early.

They will make decisions quickly.

They will maintain accountability.

They will measure outcomes.

They will build execution capabilities that endure beyond individual transactions.

Strategy identifies the destination.

Execution determines the journey.

Value realization determines whether the destination was worth pursuing in the first place.

Because strategy may define the opportunity.

But execution determines whether value is ever realized.

PART II - UNDERSTANDING VALUE REALIZATION

If execution is the problem, value realization is the objective.

Organizations do not pursue acquisitions, divestitures, technology implementations, transformations, or strategic initiatives simply to complete projects. They pursue them to create measurable improvements in performance, capability, growth, efficiency, and enterprise value. Yet many organizations focus heavily on activities, milestones, and deliverables while giving far less attention to the outcomes those activities are intended to produce.

Enterprise Value Realization represents a different way of thinking. It shifts the focus from completing work to creating outcomes, from measuring activities to measuring benefits, and from managing projects to realizing value. It recognizes that value is not created when a transaction closes, a system goes live, or a project ends. Value is realized when expected benefits become measurable, sustainable, and embedded within the organization.

The chapters in this section introduce the principles that support Enterprise Value Realization. They define what value realization means, examine the science behind successful execution, and explore the lifecycle through which value is created, protected, and sustained. Understanding these concepts provides the foundation for the execution disciplines and organizational capabilities that follow.

Because before organizations can consistently realize value, they must first understand what value realization truly means.

And they must recognize that execution is not simply about completing work.

It is about delivering outcomes.

Chapter 5 - Defining Enterprise Value Realization

For decades, organizations have measured success using familiar milestones.

The transaction closes.

The system goes live.

The project finishes.

The transition ends.

The integration team disbands.

The budget is met.

The schedule is achieved.

The final report is issued.

These events are often treated as evidence of success.

Yet many organizations discover that the expected benefits never fully materialize.

Synergies remain unrealized.

Costs remain elevated.

Revenue opportunities fail to emerge.

Operational improvements are delayed.

Technology investments underperform.

Employees struggle to adapt.

Customers experience disruption.

The organization completes the work but fails to realize the value.

This distinction is important.

Completion is not realization.

Activity is not value.

Delivery is not outcome.

These differences form the foundation of what can be described as Enterprise Value Realization.

The Traditional View of Success

Organizations have historically approached transactions and major transformations through three primary disciplines.

Strategy determines what the organization intends to achieve.

Project management coordinates the activities required to deliver change.

Financial management measures performance after implementation.

Each discipline provides value.

However, gaps often exist between them.

Strategy establishes expectations.

Projects execute activities.

Finance measures results.

But who ensures that expected value is actually achieved?

Who owns the benefits?

Who protects the synergies?

Who identifies emerging value risks?

Who measures whether outcomes are materializing?

Too often, the answer is no one.

As responsibilities transition from one group to another, accountability becomes fragmented. Teams complete their assignments and move on. Leadership attention shifts toward the next priority.

Value becomes everyone's responsibility.

Which often means it becomes no one's responsibility.

Defining Enterprise Value Realization

Enterprise Value Realization is the discipline of intentionally protecting, delivering, measuring, and sustaining value throughout the entire lifecycle of a transaction, transformation, or strategic initiative.

It recognizes that value creation does not occur at a single moment.

Value is created through a series of decisions, actions, behaviors, and outcomes that occur over time.

Enterprise Value Realization asks several fundamental questions:

- What value are we trying to achieve?

- What threatens that value?
- How will value be measured?
- Who owns the expected benefits?
- What leading indicators should be monitored?
- How will risks be identified?
- How will decisions be made?
- How will outcomes be sustained?

These questions extend beyond traditional project management.

They require leadership.

They require governance.

They require accountability.

Most importantly, they require a deliberate focus on value itself.

Value Exists Throughout the Lifecycle

Organizations frequently view value as something that appears at the end of a transaction.

In reality, value exists throughout the lifecycle.

Value is created when:

- Risks are identified early.
- Decisions are made quickly.
- Resources are available.
- Technology performs effectively.
- Employees remain engaged.
- Customers experience continuity.
- Benefits are measured.
- Outcomes are sustained.

Similarly, value can be lost at every stage.

A poor decision during due diligence.

Insufficient organizational readiness.

Delayed governance decisions.

Technology failures.

Resource constraints.

Lack of accountability.

Unmeasured benefits.

Enterprise Value Realization recognizes that value is dynamic.

It must be protected continuously.

Beyond Synergies

Many transactions define value primarily through synergy targets.

Cost reductions.

Headcount savings.

Revenue improvements.

Procurement efficiencies.

While these measures remain important, they often represent only a portion of enterprise value.

Value may also include:

- Reduced operational risk.
- Improved customer experiences.
- Technology modernization.

- Enhanced capabilities.
- Organizational agility.
- Faster decision making.
- Increased resilience.
- Greater execution capacity.

Organizations that focus exclusively on financial synergies may overlook significant sources of long-term value.

Enterprise Value Realization considers both tangible and intangible outcomes.

It recognizes that sustainable value often extends beyond the original business case.

The Four Dimensions of Value

Enterprise value can generally be viewed through four dimensions.

Financial Value

Cost reductions, synergies, profitability improvements, cash flow, and shareholder returns.

Operational Value

Process improvements, efficiency gains, productivity enhancements, and performance improvements.

Organizational Value

Leadership alignment, employee engagement, decision quality, governance effectiveness, and execution capability.

Strategic Value

Market expansion, competitive advantages, technology capabilities, and long-term growth opportunities.

Successful organizations recognize that these dimensions are interconnected.

Weakness in one area often affects the others.

Value Protection

One of the most important concepts within Enterprise Value Realization is value protection.

Organizations routinely protect physical assets.

They protect financial assets.

They protect intellectual property.

They protect information.

Yet expected value frequently receives little protection.

Synergies remain unmanaged.

Benefits lack ownership.

Risks go unmonitored.

Dependencies are overlooked.

Value protection requires intentional effort.

It requires visibility.

Measurement.

Accountability.

Leadership.

Organizations that protect value consistently outperform those that assume value will occur automatically.

Value Acceleration

Enterprise Value Realization is not solely about avoiding failure.

It is also about accelerating success.

Organizations that execute effectively often realize benefits sooner.

Decisions occur faster.

Issues are resolved earlier.

Technology adoption improves.

Benefits materialize more quickly.

The timing of value matters.

A benefit achieved twelve months late may be worth substantially less than one achieved on schedule.

Execution speed influences value realization.

Organizations that reduce delays frequently improve outcomes without changing the underlying strategy.

The Role of Leadership

Enterprise Value Realization cannot be delegated.

Project teams can manage activities.

Consultants can provide expertise.

Systems can provide data.

But leadership owns value.

Leaders establish priorities.

Leaders allocate resources.

Leaders remove obstacles.

Leaders maintain accountability.

Leaders define success.

Without leadership engagement, value realization becomes difficult.

With leadership commitment, organizations create environments where execution succeeds.

A New Discipline

As organizations become more complex, the ability to realize value becomes increasingly important.

Transactions are larger.

Technology environments are more interconnected.

Organizations face greater change.

Stakeholder expectations continue to rise.

Traditional approaches focused solely on strategy or project delivery are no longer sufficient.

Organizations require a discipline that connects:

- Strategy.
- Execution.
- Technology.

- Governance.
- Risk.
- Benefits.
- Leadership.
- Outcomes.

Enterprise Value Realization provides that connection.

It establishes value as the central organizing principle for execution.

The Future of Execution

The future belongs to organizations that understand that value does not appear automatically.

Value must be defined.

Value must be protected.

Value must be measured.

Value must be sustained.

Enterprise Value Realization provides a way of thinking about execution that extends beyond projects, transactions, and individual initiatives.

It treats execution as an enterprise capability.

It recognizes value as the ultimate measure of success.

And it challenges organizations to ask a different question.

Not:

"Did we complete the project?"

Not:

"Did we close the deal?"

Not:

"Did we finish the integration?"

But rather:

"Did we realize the value we set out to create?"

Because in the end, transactions do not create value.

Projects do not create value.

Plans do not create value.

People do.

Leadership does.

Execution does.

And value is only realized when the organization intentionally delivers the outcomes it promised to achieve.

Chapter 6 - The Science of Value Realization

For decades, organizations have attempted to manage transactions and major transformations through schedules, budgets, and milestone plans.

Project managers monitor progress.

Executives review dashboards.

Finance teams measure costs.

Leadership teams assess status reports.

Despite these efforts, organizations continue to experience delayed benefits, unrealized synergies, operational disruptions, and underperforming outcomes.

This raises an important question.

If value realization is so important, why is it so difficult to measure?

The answer lies in how organizations traditionally evaluate success.

Most organizations measure activity.

Very few measure value.

The science of value realization begins by recognizing that value itself can be observed, measured, protected, and improved.

Like financial performance, operational performance, or quality management, value realization can become a discipline.

From Art to Science

Many organizations treat value realization as an outcome that either occurs or does not occur.

A transaction succeeds.

A project fails.

Benefits appear.

Synergies materialize.

This perspective suggests that value realization is largely unpredictable.

Experience suggests otherwise.

Organizations that consistently realize value often demonstrate similar characteristics:

- Strong leadership engagement.
- Effective governance.
- Clear accountability.
- Rapid decision making.
- Healthy execution capacity.
- Effective technology management.
- Benefits ownership.
- Continuous measurement.

These characteristics can be observed.

They can be measured.

They can be improved.

This transforms value realization from an art into a science.

Leading Indicators and Lagging Indicators

One of the most important concepts within value realization is the distinction between leading indicators and lagging indicators.

Lagging indicators measure what has already happened.

Examples include:

- Realized synergies.
- Financial performance.
- Cost reductions.
- Revenue growth.
- Return on investment.
- Budget performance.

These measures are important.

However, they often appear months after problems have developed.

By the time lagging indicators deteriorate, recovery may be difficult.

Leading indicators provide earlier signals.

Examples include:

- Decision cycle times.
- Resource availability.
- Issue aging.
- Risk trends.
- Executive participation.
- Dependency health.
- Schedule volatility.
- Benefits ownership.

Leading indicators help organizations identify problems before value is lost.

They provide opportunities to intervene early.

Organizations that monitor leading indicators frequently detect execution risks before they become financial problems.

The Value Equation

Value realization can be viewed as a relationship between expected value and realized value.

Expected Value

- Synergies.
- Revenue improvements.
- Cost reductions.
- Strategic benefits.
- Operational improvements.

Realized Value

- Actual outcomes.
- Measured benefits.
- Sustained improvements.
- Financial performance.

The difference between these two conditions represents value leakage.

This relationship can be expressed simply:

Expected Value – Value Leakage = Realized Value

Organizations often focus on increasing expected value.

They seek larger synergies.

Greater savings.

More ambitious goals.

However, improving realized value frequently depends more on reducing leakage than increasing expectations.

Protecting value can be more important than creating additional assumptions.

The Value Realization Curve

Value rarely appears immediately.

Most transactions follow a recognizable pattern.

Initially, disruption occurs.

Organizations experience uncertainty.

Employees adjust.

Systems change.

Processes evolve.

Performance may temporarily decline.

As execution progresses, value begins to emerge.

Benefits accelerate.

Capabilities improve.

Costs decline.

Operations stabilize.

Eventually, realized value approaches expected value.

The shape of this curve depends heavily upon execution quality.

Strong execution accelerates value.

Poor execution delays or reduces value.

Organizations that understand this pattern can better manage expectations and identify risks.

Measuring Execution Health

Traditional project management often focuses on completed activities.

Value realization requires measuring execution health.

Execution health reflects the organization's ability to deliver expected outcomes.

Examples include:

Leadership Health

- Executive engagement.
- Decision speed.
- Accountability.

Organizational Health

- Resource availability.
- Employee engagement.
- Capacity.

Governance Health

- Issue resolution.
- Escalation effectiveness.
- Decision clarity.

Technology Health

- System readiness.
- Data quality.
- Integration stability.

Benefits Health

- Benefit ownership.
- Measurement effectiveness.
- Performance trends.

These factors influence future outcomes.

Organizations that monitor execution health gain greater visibility into emerging risks.

The Importance of Benefits Ownership

One of the most common causes of unrealized value is unclear ownership.

Synergies may exist within the business case.

Benefits may appear within presentations.

Savings may be discussed during leadership meetings.

Yet no individual owns the outcome.

Questions often remain unanswered.

Who is responsible?

How is success measured?

When should benefits appear?

What actions are required?

Benefits without owners rarely become reality.

Successful organizations assign ownership.

They establish accountability.

They monitor performance.

They review progress.

Value realization requires both measurement and responsibility.

The Role of Value Assurance

Organizations routinely audit financial controls.

They monitor safety performance.

They evaluate quality.

They assess cybersecurity.

Yet few organizations perform regular assessments of value realization.

This creates a significant gap.

Value assurance provides a mechanism for evaluating whether value remains protected throughout execution.

Value assurance examines:

- Benefits realization.
- Risk trends.
- Leadership engagement.
- Decision effectiveness.
- Organizational readiness.
- Execution health.

- Value leakage indicators.

Rather than waiting for financial results, value assurance provides early visibility.

It enables intervention before problems become irreversible.

Value assurance transforms value realization from a retrospective activity into a proactive discipline.

Learning Organizations

The science of value realization also requires learning.

Organizations frequently repeat the same mistakes.

Delayed decisions.

Resource shortages.

Technology problems.

Unclear accountability.

Benefits that are never measured.

Lessons learned are often documented but rarely institutionalized.

Organizations that improve value realization create feedback loops.

They analyze outcomes.

They identify patterns.

They refine processes.

They improve governance.

They strengthen capabilities.

Over time, execution itself becomes a competitive advantage.

The Future of Measurement

Emerging technologies are creating new opportunities.

Advanced analytics.

Predictive indicators.

Artificial intelligence.

Machine learning.

Data visualization.

Organizations increasingly possess the ability to identify risks earlier, recognize patterns, and predict outcomes.

These technologies do not replace leadership.

They improve visibility.

They strengthen decision making.

They enhance value protection.

The future of value realization will increasingly combine human judgment with analytical insight.

Organizations will move beyond measuring what happened.

They will begin predicting what is likely to happen.

The Discipline of Value Realization

Science begins with observation.

It develops through measurement.

It improves through learning.

Value realization follows the same path.

Organizations can observe execution.

They can measure leading indicators.

They can identify value leakage.

They can assess execution health.

They can improve outcomes.

The realization that value can be measured changes everything.

Execution becomes visible.

Risks become identifiable.

Benefits become manageable.

Outcomes become more predictable.

Value realization becomes a discipline.

And organizations that master this discipline gain something increasingly valuable.

The ability to consistently turn strategic intentions into measurable results.

Because value is not an accident.

It is not luck.

It is not timing.

Value realization is the product of leadership, measurement, accountability, and disciplined execution.

And like any discipline, it can be learned, strengthened, and improved.

Chapter 7 - The Value Realization Lifecycle

Most organizations view transactions and transformations as a sequence of activities.

The opportunity is identified.

The transaction closes.

The project is completed.

The integration ends.

The team disbands.

The organization moves forward.

While these milestones are important, they often create an incomplete view of how value is created.

Value does not appear at a single moment.

It develops throughout a lifecycle.

It can be strengthened.

It can be accelerated.

It can be protected.

It can also be lost.

Understanding where value is created, where risk emerges, and where leadership attention is required is essential to successful execution.

The Value Realization Lifecycle provides a framework for understanding how organizations move from strategic intent to measurable outcomes.

Value Is a Journey

Organizations frequently speak of value as if it is an event.

The deal creates value.

The system creates value.

The project creates value.

The transformation creates value.

In reality, these events only create the possibility of value.

Actual value emerges through a series of activities, decisions, behaviors, and outcomes that occur over time.

A transaction announcement creates expectations.

Execution determines outcomes.

Benefits confirm whether value has been realized.

The journey matters.

Organizations that focus only on closing, implementation, or completion often discover that value remains elusive.

The organizations that consistently realize value understand that every phase of execution influences the outcome.

Phase One: Opportunity and Strategic Intent

Every transaction or transformation begins with an opportunity.

Growth.

Market expansion.

Operational improvement.

Technology modernization.

Cost reduction.

Competitive advantage.

Strategic objectives establish expectations for the future.

Financial models estimate benefits.

Business cases justify investments.

Leadership teams define success.

At this stage, expected value is created.

However, expected value is not yet realized value.

Organizations often become highly focused on the attractiveness of the opportunity while spending less time evaluating their ability to execute it.

The quality of strategic intent remains important.

But execution capability ultimately determines whether those expectations become reality.

Phase Two: Readiness and Assessment

Before execution begins, organizations must understand their own readiness.

Questions become critically important:

- Does the organization possess sufficient capacity?
- Are leaders aligned?
- Are resources available?
- What risks exist?
- What dependencies must be managed?
- Are the expected benefits realistic?
- Is the organization prepared for change?

This phase is often overlooked.

Organizations frequently conduct extensive due diligence on the target organization while performing little assessment of themselves.

Yet organizational readiness strongly influences outcomes.

Leadership capacity.

Technology readiness.

Organizational alignment.

Decision-making effectiveness.

Execution capability.

These factors determine whether the organization can successfully absorb change.

Many value realization challenges originate long before execution begins.

Phase Three: Execution

Execution represents the longest and most demanding phase of the lifecycle.

Plans become actions.

Decisions become commitments.

Organizations begin implementing change.

During this phase, leaders must manage:

- Governance.
- Risks.
- Dependencies.
- Resources.
- Communication.
- Technology.
- Organizational change.
- Decision making.

Execution is where strategy encounters reality.

Unexpected issues emerge.

Priorities compete.

Schedules change.

Teams become stretched.

Decisions become difficult.

The quality of execution often determines the ultimate level of value achieved.

Organizations that maintain discipline, accountability, and leadership engagement during this phase consistently outperform those that do not.

Phase Four: Technology Enablement

Technology has become deeply integrated into virtually every transaction and transformation.

Systems support operations.

Data supports decisions.

Applications enable processes.

Infrastructure supports business continuity.

Technology is no longer simply a supporting function.

It is a value driver.

Technology problems frequently create some of the largest sources of value leakage:

- Data migration failures.
- System delays.
- Cybersecurity concerns.
- Integration issues.
- Application dependencies.

Successful organizations recognize that technology readiness significantly influences value realization.

Technology must enable execution rather than constrain it.

Phase Five: Transition and Stabilization

Eventually, organizations move beyond implementation activities.

Temporary structures begin to dissolve.

Transition service agreements conclude.

Integration teams disband.

New operating models emerge.

Ownership transfers to the business.

This transition period can be particularly dangerous.

Organizations often declare victory too early.

Resources are reassigned.

Leadership attention shifts.

Benefits remain unmeasured.

Without careful management, value can continue leaking long after the project appears complete.

Stabilization requires:

- Clear ownership.
- Operational accountability.
- Organizational adoption.
- Performance measurement.
- Ongoing leadership attention.

Value must survive the transition from project to operation.

Phase Six: Benefits Realization

Benefits realization represents the ultimate objective of the lifecycle.

This phase answers the most important question:

Did the organization achieve the value it expected?

Organizations measure:

- Synergies.
- Financial performance.
- Operational improvements.
- Cost reductions.
- Revenue growth.
- Productivity gains.
- Strategic outcomes.

Unfortunately, many organizations stop measuring before benefits appear.

Teams disband.

Projects close.

Budgets end.

The organization moves on.

Yet value realization often continues for months or years after implementation activities conclude.

Benefits realization requires persistence.

Measurement.

Accountability.

Ownership.

Leadership.

Without these elements, expected value frequently remains unrealized.

Value Moves Both Directions

An important characteristic of the Value Realization Lifecycle is that value can either increase or decrease at every phase.

Value grows when:

- Risks are identified early.
- Decisions occur quickly.
- Resources remain available.
- Leadership remains engaged.
- Technology performs effectively.
- Benefits are measured.

Value declines when:

- Decisions are delayed.
- Risks remain unresolved.
- Resources become constrained.
- Accountability weakens.
- Technology problems emerge.
- Benefits go unmeasured.

Value realization is not automatic.

It is dynamic.

Organizations influence it continuously.

The Importance of Continuous Assurance

Because value can change throughout the lifecycle, organizations require ongoing visibility.

They must understand:

- Where risks exist.
- Which benefits are threatened.
- Where execution health is declining.
- Which decisions require attention.

- Whether value remains protected.

This requires continuous evaluation rather than periodic review.

Organizations that maintain visibility throughout the lifecycle often identify issues before significant value loss occurs.

They intervene earlier.

They recover faster.

They protect expected outcomes.

Value realization is not a one-time assessment.

It is a continuous process.

The Emerging Lifecycle of Execution

As organizations become more complex, the lifecycle itself continues to evolve.

Artificial intelligence.

Advanced analytics.

Predictive indicators.

Execution health monitoring.

Benefits dashboards.

Digital decision support.

These capabilities increasingly allow organizations to observe value realization in real time.

The future of execution will involve:

- Earlier risk identification.
- Better decision support.
- Improved measurement.
- Greater transparency.
- Faster intervention.

Organizations will increasingly manage value as an enterprise asset.

From Lifecycle to Capability

The Value Realization Lifecycle is more than a sequence of phases.

It represents a different way of thinking about execution.

Rather than viewing transactions as projects, organizations begin viewing value realization as a continuous capability.

Opportunity.

Readiness.

Execution.

Technology.

Transition.

Benefits.

Each phase contributes to the final outcome.

Each phase contains opportunities to protect value.

Each phase presents risks that can reduce it.

The organizations that consistently realize value understand that execution does not begin at closing and end at implementation.

It begins with strategic intent.

It continues through every decision.

And it concludes only when the expected value has been fully realized.

Because value is not created at a single moment.

It is created throughout the entire lifecycle of execution.

PART III - THE FIVE PILLARS OF VALUE REALIZATION

The ability to realize enterprise value does not depend upon a single methodology, a single leader, or a single function. Organizations that consistently achieve their objectives recognize that value realization is a system comprised of multiple interconnected disciplines working together toward a common purpose.

Over decades of leading mergers, acquisitions, divestitures, technology transformations, and enterprise programs, one lesson has become increasingly clear: organizations struggle when they focus on only one aspect of execution while neglecting the others. Strong governance cannot overcome poor leadership. Exceptional technology cannot compensate for organizational misalignment. Detailed plans cannot succeed without readiness, accountability, and sustainable transition.

The AVA Enterprise Value Realization System addresses this challenge through five integrated pillars.

AVA Assess™ establishes the foundation by evaluating readiness, risk, opportunity, and the conditions necessary for success. AVA Execute™ provides the structure, governance, accountability, and operational discipline required to deliver results. AVA Lead™ focuses on leadership alignment, communication, organizational readiness, and guiding people through change. AVA Tech™ ensures that technology enables value through systems, data, cybersecurity, and digital capabilities. AVA Exit™ protects long-term value by preparing the organization for transition, sustainability, and the successful completion of transformation efforts.

These pillars do not operate independently. They reinforce one another throughout the lifecycle of a transaction, transformation, or strategic initiative. Weakness in any one pillar creates risk across the entire system.

Supporting these pillars are two enterprise-wide capabilities that span the entire framework. AVA Intelligence™ provides predictive insights, analytics, and decision support that help organizations identify risks and opportunities before they become visible. AVA Assure™ provides continuous value assurance through independent reviews, performance validation, benefits realization, and executive oversight.

Together, these capabilities form an integrated approach to enterprise value realization. The chapters in this section explore each pillar in detail, providing practical guidance, proven methodologies, and real-world lessons that help organizations move from strategy to execution and ultimately from execution to realized value.

Chapter 8 - AVA Assess™: Readiness Determines Success

Most organizations devote extraordinary effort to evaluating the transaction.

Far fewer devote the same effort to evaluating themselves.

Financial due diligence is performed.

Legal reviews are completed.

Technology assessments are conducted.

Commercial assumptions are tested.

Valuations are scrutinized.

Risks associated with the target organization are examined in detail.

Yet one of the most important questions frequently remains unanswered.

Is the organization prepared to execute?

This question lies at the heart of readiness.

And readiness often determines whether value will ultimately be realized.

The Missing Assessment

Organizations routinely evaluate:

- Financial performance.
- Operational capabilities.
- Technology environments.

- Market opportunities.
- Regulatory risks.
- Contractual obligations.

However, they seldom evaluate their own ability to absorb change.

Questions such as these often receive little attention:

- Does the organization have sufficient capacity?
- Are leaders aligned?
- Are decision rights clear?
- Are critical resources available?
- Are competing initiatives creating risk?
- Is technology prepared?
- Is governance established?
- Are benefits realistic?

Many organizations discover the answers only after execution begins.

By then, corrective actions become significantly more difficult.

The objective of readiness assessment is not to predict every problem.

It is to identify the conditions that influence successful execution.

Readiness Is a Leading Indicator

One of the most important lessons from decades of transaction experience is that outcomes often become visible long before results appear.

Organizations showing signs of:

- Leadership misalignment.
- Resource shortages.
- Unclear accountability.

- Weak governance.
- Technology uncertainty.
- Organizational fatigue.

frequently experience execution challenges later.

Conversely, organizations demonstrating:

- Strong leadership engagement.
- Available capacity.
- Clear ownership.
- Effective governance.
- Realistic expectations.
- Organizational alignment.

often execute more successfully.

Readiness is therefore a leading indicator.

It provides visibility into future execution performance.

Organizations that assess readiness early frequently identify risks before value begins to leak.

The Capacity Assessment

Chapter 3 introduced the concept of execution capacity.

Capacity remains one of the most overlooked variables in transaction success.

Organizations frequently assume:

- The business will support the effort.
- Resources will become available.
- Subject matter experts will participate.
- Leaders will have sufficient time.
- Existing workloads can continue unchanged.

These assumptions often prove incorrect.

Assessing capacity requires evaluating:

Leadership Capacity

Can leaders support both daily operations and major transformation activities?

Functional Capacity

Do critical business functions possess sufficient resources?

Subject Matter Expertise

Are key personnel available when needed?

Organizational Bandwidth

How many initiatives are competing simultaneously?

Decision Capacity

Can leadership teams make timely decisions?

Capacity constraints often emerge long before execution problems become visible.

Organizations that identify these limitations early can take corrective action.

Leadership Alignment

Successful execution requires more than executive sponsorship.

It requires alignment.

Leadership teams must agree upon:

- Strategic objectives.
- Success criteria.
- Priorities.
- Decision rights.
- Risk tolerance.
- Expected outcomes.

Misalignment frequently creates:

- Conflicting messages.
- Delayed decisions.
- Competing priorities.
- Organizational confusion.

Employees quickly recognize when leaders disagree.

Execution slows.

Accountability weakens.

Value leakage begins.

Assessing leadership alignment helps organizations identify these issues before they affect performance.

Organizational Readiness

Readiness extends beyond leadership.

Organizations themselves must be prepared for change.

This includes:

- Cultural readiness.
- Employee engagement.
- Communication effectiveness.
- Change capacity.
- Organizational resilience.

- Historical performance.

Some organizations absorb change effectively.

Others struggle with relatively modest disruptions.

Understanding these differences allows leaders to develop realistic plans and expectations.

Ignoring organizational readiness often creates unnecessary risk.

Technology Readiness

Technology increasingly determines execution success.

Systems support operations.

Applications enable processes.

Data drives decisions.

Infrastructure supports business continuity.

Organizations must understand:

- System dependencies.
- Data quality.
- Cybersecurity risks.
- Integration complexity.
- Technical resource availability.
- Technology debt.

Technology readiness frequently influences schedules, costs, and operational performance.

Assessing these conditions early improves outcomes.

Risk Visibility

Traditional risk management often focuses on individual issues.

Readiness assessment focuses on conditions.

Examples include:

- Limited capacity.
- Unclear ownership.
- Weak governance.
- Inexperienced teams.
- Leadership turnover.
- Competing priorities.
- Technology uncertainty.

These conditions may not yet represent problems.

However, they increase the likelihood that problems will emerge.

Identifying these conditions allows organizations to intervene before risks materialize.

The Readiness Scorecard

Organizations often ask whether readiness can be measured.

The answer is yes.

Examples of readiness indicators include:

Leadership

- Executive engagement.
- Decision speed.
- Alignment.

Capacity

- Resource availability.

- Competing initiatives.
- Workload levels.

Governance

- Decision rights.
- Escalation processes.
- Accountability.

Technology

- System readiness.
- Resource availability.
- Dependency health.

Organization

- Change capacity.
- Employee readiness.
- Communication effectiveness.

These indicators provide visibility into execution risk.

They help leadership teams move beyond intuition and anecdotal observations.

Readiness and Value Protection

Readiness assessments are not intended to delay decisions.

They exist to protect value.

Organizations often move quickly to pursue opportunities.

Speed remains important.

However, speed without readiness can increase risk.

Readiness enables better decisions.

It improves resource planning.

It strengthens governance.

It reduces surprises.

Most importantly, it protects value before execution begins.

The cost of assessing readiness is almost always lower than the cost of correcting execution failures.

The Emergence of AVA Assess™

Over time, the need to evaluate readiness systematically led to the development of what became known as AVA Assess™.

AVA Assess™ is built upon a simple principle:

Organizations should understand their ability to execute before execution begins.

The purpose is not to create additional process.

The purpose is to provide visibility.

Readiness.

Capacity.

Leadership alignment.

Technology preparedness.

Risk.

Organizational health.

These factors influence every subsequent phase of value realization.

Organizations that understand themselves execute differently.

They identify risks earlier.

They allocate resources more effectively.

They establish realistic expectations.

They protect value.

Readiness Determines Success

Many organizations assume that strategy determines outcomes.

Others believe execution alone determines success.

Experience suggests something different.

Readiness determines whether execution can succeed.

Organizations that begin execution without understanding their capacity, leadership alignment, organizational health, and technology readiness often encounter avoidable problems.

Organizations that assess these conditions gain advantages.

They make better decisions.

They establish stronger governance.

They prepare their teams.

They protect expected value.

The first question leaders should ask is not:

"What are we trying to accomplish?"

The second question should not be:

"How quickly can we begin?"

The most important question may be:

"Are we prepared to execute successfully?"

Because readiness does not guarantee success.

But a lack of readiness frequently guarantees difficulty.

And the organizations that consistently realize value are often the organizations that understand themselves before they attempt to change themselves.

Chapter 9 - AVA Execute™: Execution Determines Value

Organizations rarely fail because they lack intelligence.

They rarely fail because they lack strategy.

They rarely fail because they lack ambition.

Most organizations possess capable leaders, talented employees, experienced advisors, sophisticated technology, and well-developed plans.

Yet many still fail to realize the value they expect.

The difference is execution.

Execution is where strategy becomes reality.

Execution is where decisions become actions.

Execution is where benefits become measurable.

Execution is where value is either protected or lost.

This is the central principle of Enterprise Value Realization.

Execution determines value.

The Moment Strategy Ends

Strategy defines what an organization intends to accomplish.

Execution determines whether it actually happens.

The strategic plan may identify opportunities.

The financial model may estimate benefits.

The acquisition thesis may describe future value.

The transformation roadmap may define objectives.

However, none of these activities produce value.

Value begins when organizations act.

The transaction closes.

The integration starts.

The teams mobilize.

The work begins.

At that moment, strategy becomes execution.

The quality of execution now determines the outcome.

The Execution Gap

Most organizations experience a gap between intention and performance.

This gap appears in many forms.

- Expected synergies versus realized synergies.
- Planned schedules versus actual schedules.
- Estimated savings versus actual savings.
- Strategic objectives versus operational outcomes.
- Executive expectations versus organizational reality.

The larger this gap becomes, the greater the loss of value.

Many organizations attempt to close this gap through additional planning.

More meetings.

More reports.

More presentations.

More analyses.

While planning remains important, the real challenge lies elsewhere.

Execution requires action.

Execution requires accountability.

Execution requires decisions.

Execution requires leadership.

Execution Is an Enterprise Capability

Many organizations view execution as a project management function.

Execution teams manage schedules.

Project managers coordinate activities.

Workstreams complete tasks.

Status reports are produced.

These activities are necessary.

But execution extends far beyond project management.

Execution involves:

- Leadership.
- Governance.
- Accountability.
- Decision making.
- Resource allocation.
- Risk management.
- Organizational alignment.
- Technology coordination.
- Benefits realization.

Execution is not a temporary activity.

It is an enterprise capability.

Organizations that consistently execute well develop systems, behaviors, and disciplines that endure beyond individual transactions.

They institutionalize execution.

Leadership and Execution

Execution begins with leadership.

Leaders establish priorities.

Leaders make decisions.

Leaders remove obstacles.

Leaders allocate resources.

Leaders maintain accountability.

When leadership engagement declines, execution often suffers.

Decision queues develop.

Issues remain unresolved.

Teams lose direction.

Priorities compete.

Value begins to leak.

Leadership does not end when the transaction closes.

Leadership becomes even more important after execution begins.

The organizations that realize value maintain leadership attention throughout the lifecycle.

Governance Drives Performance

Execution requires structure.

Without governance:

- Decisions are delayed.
- Accountability becomes unclear.
- Escalations stall.
- Risks increase.
- Teams become misaligned.

Effective governance provides:

- Decision rights.
- Accountability.
- Escalation processes.
- Reporting structures.
- Leadership visibility.

Governance does not create bureaucracy.

Good governance removes barriers.

It accelerates decisions.

It improves alignment.

It protects value.

Organizations that govern effectively execute more effectively.

Accountability Creates Results

Many organizations struggle because responsibility becomes fragmented.

Everyone contributes.

No one owns.

Benefits belong to the organization.

Risks belong to the team.

Issues belong to the project.

Eventually, ownership disappears.

Execution requires accountability.

Somebody must own:

- The decision.
- The benefit.
- The risk.
- The milestone.
- The outcome.

Clear accountability improves speed.

It improves quality.

It improves execution.

Organizations that consistently realize value establish ownership early and maintain it throughout the lifecycle.

Decision Velocity

Execution moves at the speed of decisions.

Every transaction requires hundreds of decisions.

Operating models.

Technology platforms.

Organization structures.

Processes.

Policies.

Investments.

Resources.

The organizations that make decisions quickly often outperform those that delay.

Delayed decisions create:

- Schedule impacts.
- Resource conflicts.
- Dependency issues.
- Increased risks.
- Organizational uncertainty.

Decision velocity has become a competitive advantage.

Fast decisions do not guarantee good outcomes.

But slow decisions frequently create poor ones.

Managing Enterprise Dependencies

Modern organizations are highly interconnected.

Technology affects operations.

Operations affect customers.

Customers affect revenue.

Leadership decisions affect every function.

Few activities occur in isolation.

Execution therefore requires active dependency management.

Questions become important:

- What activities depend upon one another?
- What decisions create downstream impacts?
- Which teams influence multiple outcomes?
- Where are the bottlenecks?

Organizations frequently underestimate dependencies.

When one activity slips, several others follow.

Managing dependencies improves predictability.

It reduces surprises.

It protects value.

Execution Requires Visibility

Organizations cannot manage what they cannot see.

Execution visibility includes:

- Risks.
- Issues.
- Decisions.
- Dependencies.
- Capacity.
- Benefits.
- Performance.

Many organizations discover problems too late.

Issues remain hidden.

Risks go unreported.

Benefits are assumed.

By the time financial performance declines, recovery becomes difficult.

Execution visibility provides early warning.

It enables intervention.

It improves leadership decision making.

Visibility protects value.

The Emergence of AVA Execute™

Over time, these lessons evolved into what became AVA Execute™.

AVA Execute™ is built upon a straightforward principle:

Execution is the primary determinant of value realization.

The objective is not simply to manage projects.

The objective is to create conditions that allow organizations to execute successfully.

This includes:

- Leadership alignment.
- Governance.
- Accountability.
- Decision velocity.
- Dependency management.
- Risk visibility.
- Execution discipline.

Execution becomes a system.

A capability.

A competitive advantage.

Organizations that execute consistently outperform organizations that rely solely on strategy.

Building an Execution-First Organization

Historically, many organizations have been strategy-first organizations.

They prioritize planning.

They emphasize analysis.

They focus on opportunity identification.

The future belongs to execution-first organizations.

Execution-first organizations:

- Invest in governance.
- Develop leaders.
- Build capacity.
- Improve decision making.
- Measure benefits.
- Protect value.
- Learn continuously.

They recognize that the ability to execute repeatedly is more valuable than any individual transaction.

Execution becomes part of the culture.

Part of leadership.

Part of the operating model.

Execution Determines Value

Organizations often ask why similar strategies produce different outcomes.

Why one acquisition succeeds while another struggles.

Why one transformation accelerates performance while another disappoints.

The answer is frequently execution.

Execution determines whether risks are addressed.

Execution determines whether decisions occur.

Execution determines whether technology enables change.

Execution determines whether benefits appear.

Execution determines whether value survives.

The transaction may create the opportunity.

The strategy may establish the vision.

The financial model may estimate the outcome.

But execution determines the result.

Because value is not realized when the deal closes.

It is realized when leaders decide, teams deliver, organizations adapt, and benefits appear.

Strategy identifies the destination.

Execution determines whether the organization arrives.

And ultimately, execution determines value.

Chapter 10 - AVA Lead™: Leadership Determines Execution

Organizations often believe that execution problems are operational problems.

Schedules slip.

Actions remain open.

Decisions are delayed.

Resources become constrained.

Milestones are missed.

Benefits fail to materialize.

When these problems occur, organizations frequently respond by adding additional meetings, increasing reporting requirements, implementing new tools, or creating more detailed plans.

Yet in many cases, the root cause is not operational.

It is leadership.

Throughout my career, I have observed organizations with exceptional strategies, highly capable teams, and substantial financial resources struggle to achieve their objectives. At the same time, I have seen organizations facing difficult circumstances consistently deliver results.

The difference was often leadership.

Leadership determines priorities.

Leadership establishes accountability.

Leadership aligns organizations.

Leadership makes decisions.

Leadership creates confidence.

Leadership determines whether execution succeeds.

This is the foundation of AVA Lead™.

AVA Lead™ recognizes that successful value realization depends upon leaders who can align people, guide organizations through uncertainty, and create the conditions necessary for execution.

Leadership is not separate from execution.

Leadership enables execution.

The Leadership Gap

Many organizations underestimate the importance of leadership during major transformations.

Executives approve the initiative.

Governance structures are established.

Teams are assigned.

Plans are developed.

The assumption is that leadership involvement can decrease once execution begins.

Experience suggests otherwise.

Leadership absence creates uncertainty.

Uncertainty creates delays.

Delays create risk.

Risk creates value leakage.

Transformation places extraordinary demands on organizations. Employees face changing priorities, evolving responsibilities, increased workloads, and uncertain futures. Teams often look to leaders for direction, confidence, and clarity.

When leadership engagement declines, execution suffers.

Common leadership failures include:

- Conflicting executive priorities.
- Delayed decisions.
- Inconsistent messaging.
- Limited stakeholder engagement.
- Unclear accountability.
- Avoidance of difficult conversations.
- Lack of visible sponsorship.

Organizations often experience execution problems that are actually leadership problems.

Leadership Across the Five Pillars

Leadership influences every component of the AVA Enterprise Value Realization System.

AVA Assess™

Leaders establish the willingness to ask difficult questions.

They encourage honest assessments of risk, readiness, organizational capacity, and complexity.

Strong leaders seek the truth, even when the answers are uncomfortable.

AVA Execute™

Leaders establish accountability.

They remove obstacles.

They make decisions.

They reinforce priorities.

Execution improves when leadership remains actively engaged.

AVA Lead™

This pillar focuses directly on:

- Executive alignment.
- Organizational readiness.
- Communication.
- Stakeholder engagement.
- Change leadership.
- Decision support.
- Leadership accountability.

Successful transformations require leaders who can guide people through uncertainty.

AVA Tech™

Technology decisions increasingly influence enterprise value.

Leaders help align technology priorities with business objectives while ensuring that technology remains an enabler rather than an obstacle.

AVA Exit™

Transitions require leadership.

Ownership must be transferred.

Organizations must stabilize.

Value must be sustained.

Leaders play a critical role in ensuring that temporary solutions do not become permanent problems.

Decision Velocity

One of the most visible indicators of leadership effectiveness is decision velocity.

Organizations rarely fail because they make too many decisions.

They fail because they make decisions too slowly.

Delayed decisions create:

- Schedule delays.
- Resource conflicts.
- Organizational frustration.
- Increased costs.
- Reduced confidence.

Effective leaders understand that imperfect decisions made at the appropriate time often create better outcomes than perfect decisions made too late.

Decision-making is one of the primary responsibilities of leadership.

Leadership and Organizational Alignment

Alignment is one of the most valuable leadership contributions.

Organizations frequently experience:

- Conflicting priorities.
- Competing objectives.

- Functional disagreements.
- Resource conflicts.
- Unclear ownership.

Leaders create alignment by establishing shared objectives and reinforcing common priorities.

People support what they understand.

Teams execute what leaders consistently communicate.

Organizations move in the direction leaders emphasize.

The Future of Leadership

The future of value realization will require new leadership capabilities.

Organizations are becoming:

- More complex.
- More technology dependent.
- More data driven.
- More interconnected.
- More dynamic.

Leaders must increasingly integrate:

- Business strategy.
- Execution.
- Technology.
- Organizational change.
- Value realization.

They must become translators between executives, operational teams, technology organizations, and stakeholders.

They must lead through uncertainty.

They must guide organizations through change.

They must create confidence when answers are incomplete.

AVA Intelligence™ and Leadership

Future leaders will increasingly rely upon AVA Intelligence™.

Predictive analytics, early warning indicators, trend analysis, and decision support tools provide leaders with information that previous generations never possessed.

However, intelligence does not replace leadership.

Data can identify risks.

Analytics can identify trends.

Artificial intelligence can provide recommendations.

Leaders still make decisions.

Leaders still establish priorities.

Leaders still inspire confidence.

Leadership remains a fundamentally human responsibility.

AVA Assure™ and Leadership Accountability

Leadership also requires accountability.

AVA Assure™ provides independent validation that value remains achievable.

Assurance reviews help leaders answer important questions:

- Are we realizing value?
- Are risks increasing?
- Are benefits achievable?
- Is the organization aligned?

- Are we prepared for transition?

Strong leaders welcome objective feedback.

They seek transparency.

They encourage honest assessment.

They understand that assurance protects value.

Mentoring the Next Generation

Perhaps the most important responsibility of leadership is developing future leaders.

Throughout my career, many of the lessons that shaped my understanding of leadership came from experienced professionals willing to share their knowledge, challenge my thinking, and provide guidance.

Those experiences cannot always be captured in methodologies, processes, or governance documents.

They are transferred through mentoring.

Experienced leaders become teachers.

Program leaders become coaches.

Executives become mentors.

Organizations that intentionally develop future leaders create sustainable advantages.

The next generation will face increasingly complex transformations, greater technological dependence, and higher expectations for measurable outcomes.

They will need:

- Judgment.
- Perspective.
- Experience.
- Guidance.
- Mentorship.

Leadership therefore extends beyond current results.

Leadership prepares others to succeed.

Leadership and Legacy

Many leaders measure success through projects completed, financial results, or organizational accomplishments.

While these achievements matter, legacy extends beyond the work itself.

Legacy is reflected in:

- The people developed.
- The leaders created.
- The knowledge shared.
- The lessons preserved.
- The confidence instilled.

Organizations that invest in leadership development preserve institutional knowledge and strengthen their ability to realize value in the future.

Leadership therefore becomes one of the most important value drivers within the enterprise.

Because in the end:

Strategy creates direction.

Execution creates value.

Technology enables progress.

Assurance protects outcomes.

But leadership determines whether people choose to follow.

Execution determines value.

Leadership determines execution.

And legacy determines whether that capability endures.

Chapter 11 - AVA Tech™: Technology Enables Value

For many years, technology was viewed as a supporting function within mergers, acquisitions, and major transformations.

Finance drove the business case.

Operations drove execution.

Leadership drove decisions.

Technology was expected to implement the systems necessary to support the outcome.

That view no longer reflects reality.

Today, technology influences virtually every aspect of enterprise value.

Technology supports operations.

Technology enables decisions.

Technology connects employees.

Technology serves customers.

Technology protects information.

Technology drives productivity.

Technology enables growth.

And increasingly, technology determines whether organizations successfully execute change.

Technology is no longer a workstream.

Technology is a value driver.

The Technology Reality

Modern organizations are deeply interconnected.

Applications support business processes.

Data drives decision making.

Infrastructure enables operations.

Cybersecurity protects the enterprise.

Digital capabilities influence customer experiences.

Cloud platforms support collaboration.

Automation improves efficiency.

When organizations change, technology changes.

When technology changes, the organization changes.

This relationship creates both opportunity and risk.

Successful technology execution can accelerate value realization.

Technology failures can quickly destroy it.

The Hidden Complexity of Technology

Technology environments rarely receive the attention they deserve during early planning.

Organizations often focus on:

- Synergies.
- Organizational structures.
- Operating models.
- Financial benefits.

Meanwhile, technology teams begin uncovering:

- Thousands of applications.
- Legacy systems.
- Data quality issues.
- Infrastructure dependencies.
- Cybersecurity concerns.
- Unsupported platforms.
- Integration challenges.

Complexity emerges quickly.

Many organizations underestimate:

- The number of systems involved.
- The effort required to migrate data.
- The risks associated with cutovers.
- The impact of application dependencies.
- The time required to implement change.

Technology challenges frequently become execution challenges.

And execution challenges become value challenges.

Technology and Value Leakage

Technology issues represent one of the largest sources of value leakage.

Examples include:

- Delayed system migrations.
- Failed data conversions.

- Extended transitional services agreements.
- Cybersecurity incidents.
- Integration failures.
- Reporting disruptions.
- Operational outages.

The consequences often extend far beyond the technology organization.

Operations are affected.

Customers are impacted.

Financial reporting suffers.

Decision making slows.

Employees lose confidence.

The organization experiences disruption.

Technology failures frequently create enterprise-wide consequences.

Data as an Enterprise Asset

Organizations often focus on applications.

However, data increasingly represents one of the most important assets involved in any transaction or transformation.

Data supports:

- Financial reporting.
- Operations.
- Customers.
- Regulatory compliance.
- Decision making.

- Analytics.
- Performance measurement.

Poor data quality creates risk.

Inconsistent data creates confusion.

Incomplete data affects decisions.

Many organizations discover data issues only after migration begins.

At that point, remediation becomes difficult.

Data readiness should be evaluated early.

Organizations that understand their data environments frequently execute more successfully.

Cybersecurity and Risk

Cybersecurity has become a critical component of enterprise value.

Transactions often create:

- Expanded attack surfaces.
- New access requirements.
- System connectivity.
- Data movement.
- Third-party risks.

Cybersecurity issues can delay transactions, increase costs, and expose organizations to significant operational and financial risks.

Organizations must understand:

- Security controls.
- Access management.

- Identity management.
- Vulnerabilities.
- Compliance requirements.

Security cannot be an afterthought.

It must be integrated into execution planning.

Protecting value increasingly requires protecting information.

Technology Capacity

Technology organizations face many of the same challenges discussed earlier in this book.

Lean staffing.

Competing priorities.

Limited subject matter expertise.

Existing operational responsibilities.

Technology teams are often asked to:

- Support daily operations.
- Maintain cybersecurity.
- Implement new systems.
- Support integration activities.
- Execute transformations.
- Deliver innovation initiatives.

Capacity becomes constrained.

Critical resources become bottlenecks.

Schedules slip.

Risks increase.

Technology capacity frequently determines execution capacity.

Organizations that fail to account for these limitations often experience delays.

Technology Decisions

Technology decisions often carry long-term consequences.

Examples include:

- Application selection.
- ERP strategies.
- Data architectures.
- Infrastructure models.
- Cloud adoption.
- Integration approaches.

These decisions influence:

- Costs.
- Risks.
- Scalability.
- Performance.
- Future capabilities.

Decision delays can significantly affect execution.

Organizations frequently postpone technology decisions because they appear complex.

Unfortunately, delayed technology decisions often create larger problems later.

Technology requires decision velocity.

Technology and the Operating Model

Technology is not separate from the business.

Technology enables the operating model.

Processes depend on systems.

Employees depend on applications.

Leaders depend on data.

Customers depend on digital capabilities.

Organizations frequently discuss future operating models without fully considering the technology required to support them.

A successful operating model requires:

- Appropriate systems.
- Reliable data.
- Effective integration.
- Clear ownership.
- Sustainable support.

Technology and operations must evolve together.

The Emergence of AVA Tech™

Over time, it became increasingly clear that technology deserved greater attention within value realization.

Technology was not simply a functional workstream.

It was influencing:

- Execution speed.
- Organizational readiness.

- Decision making.
- Risk.
- Benefits realization.
- Operational continuity.

This realization contributed to the development of AVA Tech™.

AVA Tech™ is built upon a straightforward principle:

Technology enables value.

The objective is not simply to implement systems.

The objective is to ensure that technology supports successful execution and long-term value realization.

This includes:

- Technology readiness.
- Application strategy.
- Data quality.
- Cybersecurity.
- Infrastructure.
- Integration.
- Operational continuity.

Technology becomes an enterprise capability.

Not merely an IT function.

The Future of Technology and Value

Technology continues to evolve rapidly.

Artificial intelligence.

Automation.

Advanced analytics.

Cloud computing.

Digital platforms.

Predictive insights.

These capabilities increasingly influence how organizations operate and compete.

Technology is no longer only supporting the business.

Technology is becoming the business.

Organizations that successfully integrate technology into execution gain advantages:

- Better decisions.
- Faster execution.
- Greater visibility.
- Improved resilience.
- Stronger performance.

Organizations that treat technology as an afterthought often experience avoidable challenges.

Technology Enables Value

Technology does not create value by itself.

Systems do not realize benefits.

Applications do not execute strategies.

Platforms do not make decisions.

People do.

Leadership does.

Execution does.

Technology enables these activities.

When technology performs effectively, organizations execute more successfully.

When technology struggles, value often suffers.

The question facing modern organizations is no longer:

"What technology do we need?"

The more important question is:

"How does technology help us realize value?"

Because in today's environment, technology is not simply part of execution.

Technology enables execution.

And execution determines value.

Chapter 12 - AVA Exit™: Transition Determines Sustainability

Many organizations believe the work is complete when the system goes live.

The integration finishes.

The transition services agreement expires.

The project team disbands.

The final status report is issued.

The budget is closed.

Leadership turns its attention elsewhere.

The organization moves forward.

Unfortunately, this is often the moment when new risks begin to emerge.

Temporary solutions become permanent.

Benefits remain unmeasured.

Processes are not fully adopted.

Operational issues appear.

Ownership becomes unclear.

The value created during execution begins to deteriorate.

The challenge is not completing the transition.

The challenge is sustaining the outcome.

Transition determines sustainability.

The Forgotten Phase

Organizations devote substantial attention to transactions, integrations, and implementations.

They establish governance.

Build project teams.

Develop plans.

Manage risks.

Execute activities.

Yet comparatively little attention is given to what happens after the work is complete.

Questions frequently remain unanswered.

- Who owns the processes?
- Who measures the benefits?
- Who supports the technology?
- Who manages unresolved risks?
- Who ensures accountability?
- Who maintains performance?

As temporary structures disappear, organizations must assume permanent ownership.

This transition is one of the most important phases of value realization.

Unfortunately, it is also one of the least understood.

Temporary Organizations

Transactions and transformations often create temporary organizations.

Integration management offices.

Program teams.

Transition teams.

Steering committees.

Workstreams.

Project structures.

These organizations exist to deliver change.

Eventually, they disappear.

However, the business itself must continue operating.

Responsibilities must transition.

Knowledge must transfer.

Capabilities must develop.

Ownership must become permanent.

When this transition is poorly managed, organizations often experience:

- Operational disruptions.
- Performance declines.
- Loss of accountability.
- Technology issues.

- Unresolved risks.
- Delayed benefits.

Execution may be complete.

Value realization is not.

The TSA Trap

Transition Services Agreements frequently illustrate this challenge.

TSAs are intended to provide temporary support.

They allow operations to continue while capabilities are developed.

They create stability during periods of change.

However, organizations often become dependent upon them.

Exit dates move.

Extensions occur.

Costs increase.

Risks accumulate.

The organization delays difficult decisions.

Temporary solutions remain in place.

Value is lost.

The problem is not the TSA itself.

The problem is the lack of transition readiness.

Successful organizations treat TSAs as temporary bridges.

Unsuccessful organizations treat them as operating models.

Operational Independence

One of the primary objectives of transition is operational independence.

Organizations must be capable of operating successfully without temporary support structures.

Operational independence includes:

- Stable processes.
- Clear ownership.
- Trained personnel.
- Technology readiness.
- Support capabilities.
- Performance measurement.
- Decision authority.

The organization must be able to function effectively under its new operating model.

Independence does not occur automatically.

It must be intentionally developed.

Knowledge Transfer

Many transitions depend upon individuals.

Subject matter experts.

Project teams.

External consultants.

Legacy personnel.

Temporary resources.

When these individuals depart, knowledge frequently departs with them.

Organizations may lose:

- Process knowledge.
- System expertise.
- Historical understanding.
- Decision context.
- Operational experience.

Knowledge transfer becomes essential.

Documentation alone is rarely sufficient.

Organizations must develop capabilities.

Train personnel.

Establish support structures.

Create sustainable ownership.

Transition succeeds when knowledge becomes institutionalized.

Organizational Adoption

New systems do not create value.

New processes do not create value.

New operating models do not create value.

Organizations create value when people adopt these changes.

Adoption frequently determines sustainability.

Questions become important:

- Are employees using the new processes?
- Are leaders supporting the changes?
- Are behaviors changing?
- Are decisions improving?
- Are new capabilities developing?

Without adoption, organizations often revert to previous behaviors.

Temporary improvements disappear.

Benefits erode.

Value leaks.

Sustainability depends upon organizational adoption.

Benefits Must Survive the Transition

Many benefits begin appearing only after execution activities have concluded.

Cost reductions.

Operational efficiencies.

Revenue improvements.

Productivity gains.

Capability development.

Organizations frequently stop measuring too early.

The project closes.

The team disbands.

Leadership attention shifts.

Yet benefits continue to emerge.

Transition therefore requires:

- Benefit ownership.
- Performance monitoring.
- Accountability.
- Ongoing measurement.

Value cannot simply be assumed.

It must be verified.

Risk Does Not End

Organizations often assume that risks decline as projects conclude.

In reality, risks frequently change.

Project risks become operational risks.

Temporary issues become permanent challenges.

Examples include:

- Unsupported systems.
- Incomplete processes.
- Staffing gaps.
- Unresolved dependencies.
- Knowledge deficiencies.
- Technology debt.

Transition requires continued visibility.

Organizations must understand:

- What remains unresolved.
- What risks continue.
- What actions are required.

Successful organizations exit responsibly.

They do not simply stop.

The Emergence of AVA Exit™

Over time, it became increasingly clear that transition deserved greater attention.

Exit was not simply the conclusion of execution.

Exit determined whether value survived.

This realization contributed to the development of AVA Exit™.

AVA Exit™ is based upon a simple principle:

Temporary execution structures must become sustainable operating capabilities.

The objective is not merely:

- Ending the TSA.
- Closing the project.
- Dissolving the team.

The objective is achieving:

- Operational independence.
- Organizational adoption.
- Sustainable ownership.
- Capability transfer.

- Long-term performance.
- Continued value realization.

Exit becomes a value discipline.

Not simply an administrative milestone.

Sustainability as a Competitive Advantage

Organizations that transition effectively realize several advantages.

They achieve:

- Faster stabilization.
- Lower operational risk.
- Improved performance.
- Better adoption.
- Stronger accountability.
- Sustainable benefits.

Organizations that struggle with transition often experience:

- Extended support costs.
- Operational disruption.
- Delayed benefits.
- Employee frustration.
- Increased risks.

The difference frequently lies in preparation.

Transition should begin long before execution ends.

Beyond the Finish Line

Many organizations view execution as a race.

The objective becomes reaching the finish line.

Completing the implementation.

Achieving the cutover.

Exiting the TSA.

Closing the project.

The reality is different.

The finish line is often where value realization truly begins.

Organizations must continue:

- Measuring benefits.
- Supporting adoption.
- Managing risks.
- Monitoring performance.
- Building capabilities.

The future organization must stand on its own.

Because execution does not end when the project closes.

Execution ends when the organization can sustain the value that has been created.

Transition Determines Sustainability

Strategy creates opportunity.

Execution delivers change.

Technology enables performance.

Transition determines whether value survives.

Organizations frequently ask:

"Did we complete the project?"

A more important question may be:

"Can the organization succeed without the project?"

Because temporary teams eventually disappear.

Consultants leave.

Programs end.

Projects close.

What remains is the business itself.

And the ultimate measure of success is not whether the transition occurred.

It is whether the organization can sustain the value that the transition was intended to create.

Because value that cannot be sustained is eventually lost.

And sustainability begins with a successful exit.

PART IV - EXECUTION LEADERSHIP

Frameworks do not execute. Processes do not execute. Technology does not execute. Organizations realize value through people, and people realize value through leadership.

Throughout this book, we have examined the challenges that prevent organizations from achieving the outcomes they seek and the execution disciplines that support value realization. Yet even the strongest frameworks, governance structures, and methodologies cannot succeed without leaders who are willing to make decisions, remove obstacles, establish accountability, and sustain organizational focus. Execution ultimately becomes a leadership responsibility.

Modern organizations operate in environments characterized by increasing complexity, accelerating change, competing priorities, and growing expectations. Leaders must make decisions with incomplete information, allocate limited resources, resolve conflicts, and maintain organizational alignment while continuing to deliver business performance. The ability to lead execution has become just as important as the ability to define strategy.

The chapters in this section examine the leadership disciplines that support successful execution. Governance creates clarity and accountability. Decision velocity creates organizational speed. Culture determines how people behave when challenges emerge. The Integration Management Office provides coordination and visibility. Together, these capabilities create the operating environment in which value realization becomes possible.

Because organizations do not realize value through frameworks alone.

They realize value through leaders who create alignment, make decisions, establish accountability, and build organizations capable of executing successfully.

And ultimately, leadership determines whether execution becomes a competitive advantage or a source of value leakage.

Chapter 13 - Risk Management for Value Realization

Every organization manages risk.

Project teams maintain risk registers.

Executives review enterprise risks.

Auditors assess controls.

Technology teams evaluate cybersecurity threats.

Compliance functions monitor regulatory exposure.

Yet despite these efforts, organizations continue to lose significant amounts of enterprise value.

The problem is not that risks are unknown.

The problem is that organizations often focus on individual risks while failing to understand the broader risks to value realization itself.

Schedules slip.

Decisions are delayed.

Leadership alignment weakens.

Technology challenges emerge.

Resources become constrained.

Transition activities stall.

Benefits fail to materialize.

Eventually, value begins to disappear.

These events rarely occur in isolation.

They interact with one another.

They compound over time.

They create enterprise value risk.

Traditional risk management often focuses on the probability and impact of individual events. While this approach remains important, organizations increasingly require a broader perspective.

They must ask:

- What threatens value?
- What could prevent benefits realization?
- Where are dependencies increasing?
- Which decisions are being delayed?
- Where is organizational alignment weakening?
- Which capabilities are becoming vulnerable?

Risk management therefore becomes a discipline of protecting value.

The AVA Enterprise Value Realization System provides a framework for understanding these risks.

AVA Assess™ Risks

Organizations frequently begin major initiatives before understanding readiness, capacity, complexity, and organizational constraints.

Common risks include:

- Incomplete due diligence.
- Unclear value drivers.
- Unrealistic assumptions.

- Insufficient resources.
- Undefined success criteria.
- Poor organizational readiness.
- Underestimated complexity.

Organizations that fail to assess honestly often begin execution already at risk.

AVA Execute™ Risks

Execution risks remain among the most visible.

These include:

- Missed milestones.
- Delayed decisions.
- Dependency failures.
- Governance weaknesses.
- Accountability gaps.
- Resource overload.
- Escalation delays.

Execution risk frequently becomes value leakage.

AVA Lead™ Risks

Leadership risk is often underestimated.

Organizations experience:

- Executive misalignment.
- Communication failures.
- Stakeholder resistance.
- Change fatigue.
- Declining morale.
- Leadership turnover.
- Unclear accountability.

People problems often become execution problems.

AVA Tech™ Risks

Technology increasingly influences every transformation.

Technology risks include:

- Data migration failures.
- Cybersecurity concerns.
- Application dependencies.
- Infrastructure constraints.
- ERP delays.
- Integration failures.
- Technology resource shortages.

Technology problems frequently become business problems.

AVA Exit™ Risks

Many organizations underestimate the importance of transition and sustainability.

Risks include:

- Delayed TSA exits.
- Unclear ownership.
- Operational instability.
- Dependency persistence.
- Incomplete knowledge transfer.
- Support model weaknesses.
- Benefits erosion.

Value can continue to leak long after a project appears complete.

These five pillars provide a more complete view of enterprise risk because they focus on the factors that directly influence value realization.

However, future organizations require additional capabilities.

AVA Intelligence™ represents the evolution from reactive risk management to predictive risk management.

Artificial intelligence, predictive analytics, trend analysis, and early warning indicators increasingly help organizations identify emerging risks before they become visible.

Examples include:

- Declining decision velocity.
- Increasing issue aging.
- Leadership disengagement.
- Resource overload trends.
- Benefit forecast deterioration.
- Dependency concentrations.
- Organizational sentiment changes.

Organizations that identify these signals early gain valuable time to respond.

At the same time, organizations require independent validation.

AVA Assure™ provides this capability.

Value assurance reviews, health assessments, governance evaluations, and benefits realization reviews allow organizations to continuously determine whether value remains achievable.

Risk management therefore becomes more than avoiding problems.

It becomes protecting value.

Yet one of the most significant risks facing organizations today receives relatively little attention.

The loss of knowledge.

Across industries, experienced professionals retire, move into new roles, or leave organizations. Decades of experience, lessons learned, relationships, and practical judgment often leave with them.

This creates institutional risk.

The loss of experienced leaders creates:

- Leadership risk.
- Execution risk.
- Decision-making risk.
- Organizational risk.
- Transition risk.

Organizations that fail to transfer knowledge often repeat the same mistakes.

Mentoring therefore becomes a form of risk management.

Experienced leaders reduce risk by developing others.

Program leaders reduce risk by sharing lessons learned.

Executives reduce risk by coaching future leaders.

Organizations reduce risk by preserving institutional knowledge.

The future of value realization depends not only upon managing projects and programs, but upon developing people who understand how to lead them.

The next generation will inherit greater complexity, increasing technological dependence, and higher expectations for measurable outcomes.

They will require:

- Judgment.
- Perspective.
- Experience.
- Guidance.

- Mentorship.

Organizations that invest in these capabilities reduce long-term risk.

Ultimately, risk management for value realization requires organizations to:

Assess honestly.

Execute with discipline.

Lead effectively.

Enable through technology.

Transition successfully.

Apply intelligence.

Provide assurance.

Develop people.

Preserve knowledge.

Build future leaders.

Because the greatest risks are often not the ones listed in a register.

They are the risks organizations fail to recognize until value has already been lost.

The organizations that succeed in the future will not simply manage risk.

They will manage value.

And they will recognize that protecting value today includes preparing others to protect it tomorrow.

Chapter 14 - Governance That Drives Results

"Governance is not about controlling execution. Governance exists to enable execution."

Most organizations believe they have governance. They have steering committees, executive meetings, project status reports, and decision logs. They have organizational charts that define reporting relationships and approval authorities. On paper, governance appears comprehensive.

Yet despite all of these structures, projects continue to miss deadlines, integrations stall, transformation programs lose momentum, and expected value never materializes.

The problem is not the absence of governance.

The problem is ineffective governance.

Too often, governance becomes an administrative exercise focused on reporting rather than decision-making. Leadership teams spend hours reviewing status updates instead of resolving the issues preventing progress. Meetings become informational rather than transformational. Risks are documented but not mitigated. Dependencies are identified but remain unresolved. Decisions are deferred until the next meeting, and every delay allows enterprise value to leak away.

Governance should never become bureaucracy.

Its purpose is to create clarity, accelerate decisions, remove obstacles, and maintain accountability. High-performing organizations understand that governance is one of the most powerful execution tools available when it is designed correctly.

Good governance does not slow execution.

It accelerates it.

Governance Exists to Enable Decisions

Every transformation program eventually encounters uncertainty. Conflicting priorities emerge. Resources become constrained. Risks evolve. New information becomes available. At these moments, execution depends less on planning and more on the organization's ability to make timely, informed decisions.

This is where governance creates value.

The best governance models establish clear decision rights before execution begins. Everyone understands which decisions belong at the executive level, which belong within the Integration Management Office, and which can be made by functional leaders. Escalation paths are defined, expectations are understood, and accountability is transparent.

When governance is clear, decision velocity increases.

When governance is unclear, organizations wait.

Waiting is expensive.

Every delayed decision increases uncertainty, creates rework, consumes leadership attention, and erodes confidence across the organization.

Governance Is About Accountability

Successful organizations do not govern activities.

They govern outcomes.

Executive governance should focus on whether the organization is realizing the value that justified the transaction in the first place. Discussions should revolve around enterprise outcomes rather than isolated project milestones.

Questions such as these become central:

- Are we realizing expected synergies?
- Where is value leaking?
- Which decisions require executive intervention?
- Which dependencies threaten our objectives?
- Are we creating additional execution capacity?
- Are benefits still achievable?

Governance shifts from monitoring work to protecting enterprise value.

Building an Effective Governance Model

An effective governance model establishes clear layers of accountability.

Executive Steering Committee

Provides strategic direction, resolves enterprise-level issues, approves major decisions, and ensures executive alignment.

Integration Management Office (IMO)

Coordinates execution across workstreams, manages dependencies, tracks risks, facilitates governance meetings, and provides enterprise-wide visibility.

Functional Leadership

Owns execution within each business function while remaining accountable for enterprise objectives rather than departmental success.

Project Teams

Deliver work, identify emerging risks, escalate issues promptly, and provide accurate execution data.

Every layer has a distinct role.

Every layer contributes to enterprise value realization.

Governance Cadence Matters

Governance is not defined by organizational charts.

It is defined by cadence.

High-performing organizations establish predictable governance rhythms that create transparency without unnecessary bureaucracy.

Typical governance activities include:

- Daily operational coordination meetings
- Weekly workstream reviews
- Weekly Integration Management Office reviews
- Bi-weekly executive steering committee meetings
- Monthly Value Assurance Reviews
- Quarterly Benefits Realization Reviews

Each meeting should have a clearly defined purpose, required decisions, expected outcomes, and measurable actions.

Meetings that do not produce decisions consume organizational capacity without creating value.

Measuring Governance Effectiveness

Organizations often measure project performance while rarely measuring governance performance.

Yet governance itself can—and should—be evaluated.

Indicators of effective governance include:

- Decision cycle time

- Escalation response time
- Risk resolution rate
- Issue aging
- Cross-functional dependency resolution
- Executive participation
- Governance action completion
- Benefits realization progress
- Stakeholder confidence

When these indicators improve, execution improves.

Governance Across the Value Realization Lifecycle

Governance evolves throughout the lifecycle.

During opportunity framing, governance focuses on strategic alignment and investment decisions.

During due diligence, it emphasizes risk identification and execution readiness.

During integration planning, governance establishes accountability, operating cadence, and decision structures.

During execution, governance removes barriers, resolves conflicts, and maintains momentum.

During stabilization and benefits realization, governance shifts toward measuring outcomes, sustaining improvements, and ensuring long-term value realization.

The governance model should evolve with the transaction—not remain static.

Governance and the Five Pillars of Value Realization

Governance connects every pillar of the AVA Enterprise Value Realization System.

AVA Assess™ evaluates governance readiness before execution begins.

AVA Execute™ relies on governance to coordinate delivery and maintain momentum.

AVA Lead™ uses governance to create executive alignment and decision velocity.

AVA Tech™ depends on governance to prioritize technology investments, manage digital risk, and coordinate technical execution.

AVA Exit™ requires governance to oversee transition planning, operational readiness, TSA exit, and sustainable operating models.

Across every pillar, governance provides the structure that transforms independent activities into coordinated enterprise execution.

Governance Drives Results

Organizations do not realize value because they hold more meetings.

They realize value because governance creates faster decisions, clearer accountability, stronger alignment, and disciplined execution.

The organizations that consistently outperform their competitors understand that governance is not an administrative necessity—it is a strategic capability.

Governance transforms complexity into clarity.

It transforms accountability into action.

Most importantly, it transforms strategy into measurable enterprise value.

Governance does not exist to monitor progress.

Governance exists to drive results.

Chapter 15 - Decision Velocity as a Competitive Advantage

Every major transaction, transformation, or strategic initiative eventually reaches the same point.

The teams are assembled.

The plans are developed.

The risks are identified.

The schedules are established.

The work begins.

And then the organization waits.

Teams wait for decisions.

Projects wait for approvals.

Risks wait for resolution.

Resources wait for direction.

Dependencies wait for answers.

Schedules wait for action.

At that moment, execution slows.

Not because the organization lacks intelligence.

Not because the strategy is flawed.

Not because the teams are incapable.

Execution slows because decisions do not occur.

Organizations execute at the speed of decisions.

The Cost of Waiting

Every transaction requires hundreds, and often thousands, of decisions.

Organization structures.

Technology platforms.

Operating models.

Application strategies.

Resource allocations.

Policy decisions.

Vendor selections.

Transition approaches.

Risk responses.

Investment priorities.

Some decisions are small.

Others influence the entire enterprise.

Regardless of size, each unresolved decision creates consequences.

Teams pause.

Dependencies accumulate.

Schedules shift.

Costs increase.

Risks expand.

Employees become frustrated.

Customers experience uncertainty.

Decision delays create value leakage.

And unlike many risks, decision delays often affect multiple workstreams simultaneously.

The Decision Bottleneck

Most organizations unintentionally create decision bottlenecks.

Executives become overloaded.

Approval processes become complex.

Authority becomes unclear.

Multiple stakeholders must agree.

Meetings are scheduled.

Presentations are developed.

Additional analysis is requested.

The intention is often good.

Leaders want to make informed decisions.

However, organizations frequently confuse additional information with improved decision quality.

At some point, delay becomes the larger risk.

A good decision made quickly often creates more value than a perfect decision made too late.

The Fear of Wrong Decisions

Many organizations delay decisions because leaders fear making mistakes.

This fear is understandable.

Transactions involve significant investments.

Transformations create organizational disruption.

Technology decisions carry long-term consequences.

Leaders want certainty.

Unfortunately, certainty rarely exists.

Execution occurs within ambiguity.

Incomplete information.

Changing conditions.

Competing priorities.

Evolving risks.

The objective is not perfect decisions.

The objective is timely decisions.

Organizations that wait for complete certainty frequently fall behind.

The Cost of No Decision

Organizations often focus on the risk of making the wrong decision.

They pay less attention to the cost of making no decision.

Delayed decisions create:

- Schedule delays.
- Resource conflicts.
- Extended costs.
- Technology impacts.
- Organizational uncertainty.
- Increased risks.

No decision is still a decision.

It is a decision to wait.

It is a decision to delay.

It is a decision to accept uncertainty.

In many cases, the cost of inaction exceeds the cost of an imperfect choice.

Decision Velocity and Value Realization

Decision velocity refers to the speed at which organizations make and implement decisions.

High decision velocity does not mean reckless decisions.

It means:

- Clear authority.
- Defined accountability.
- Available information.
- Effective governance.
- Leadership engagement.

Organizations with high decision velocity often experience:

- Faster execution.
- Lower risk.
- Improved alignment.
- Reduced delays.
- Stronger outcomes.

Organizations with low decision velocity frequently experience:

- Schedule slippage.
- Resource conflicts.
- Employee frustration.
- Increased costs.
- Value leakage.

Decision velocity influences value realization because time itself carries value.

Delayed benefits are often reduced benefits.

Leadership and Decision Making

Leaders play a central role in decision velocity.

Executives establish:

- Decision rights.
- Governance structures.
- Escalation paths.
- Risk tolerances.
- Priorities.

Leaders also model behavior.

Organizations observe:

- How quickly leaders respond.
- How willing leaders are to decide.
- How conflict is resolved.
- How accountability is reinforced.

Decision cultures emerge from leadership behavior.

Organizations that value speed, ownership, and accountability often make decisions more effectively.

Organizations that reward caution, consensus, and excessive analysis frequently move more slowly.

Decision Rights

One of the most common causes of delayed decisions is unclear authority.

Questions arise:

- Who owns the decision?
- Who provides input?
- Who approves?
- Who executes?

When decision rights remain unclear:

- Multiple people assume ownership.
- No one assumes ownership.
- Teams escalate unnecessarily.
- Decisions stall.

Clear decision rights improve speed.

They reduce confusion.

They improve accountability.

Organizations that execute effectively understand who decides.

Escalation and Resolution

Not every decision can occur at the working level.

Some require executive involvement.

Others involve risk, investment, or organizational implications.

Effective organizations establish escalation mechanisms.

Issues move quickly.

Decisions occur at the appropriate level.

Leadership intervenes when necessary.

Escalation should accelerate decisions.

Unfortunately, many organizations use escalation as a substitute for decision making.

Problems move upward.

Meetings increase.

Time passes.

Execution slows.

Escalation should remove obstacles, not create them.

Information Versus Action

Modern organizations possess more information than ever before.

Dashboards.

Analytics.

Reports.

Metrics.

Presentations.

Forecasts.

Yet more information does not always produce better decisions.

At some point, organizations must act.

The objective of information is to support decisions.

The objective of decisions is to support execution.

The objective of execution is to realize value.

Information without action creates little value.

Action without information creates unnecessary risk.

The balance between the two determines decision effectiveness.

Decision Velocity as a Competitive Advantage

Historically, organizations competed through:

- Scale.
- Capital.
- Technology.
- Market position.

Increasingly, organizations compete through speed.

The ability to:

- Recognize issues.
- Make decisions.
- Allocate resources.
- Resolve conflicts.
- Adapt quickly.

This capability creates significant advantages.

Faster organizations often:

- Capture value sooner.
- Reduce risks earlier.
- Respond to change more effectively.
- Improve employee confidence.
- Increase organizational agility.

Decision velocity becomes a strategic capability.

It influences execution.

Execution influences value.

The Role of Governance

Chapter 12 introduced governance as the operating system of execution.

Decision velocity represents one of its primary outputs.

Good governance:

- Clarifies authority.
- Establishes accountability.
- Defines escalation paths.

- Enables leadership engagement.

Poor governance creates:

- Confusion.
- Delays.
- Multiple approvals.
- Unclear ownership.

Organizations do not become faster by demanding urgency.

They become faster by improving governance.

Decision Health

Organizations can measure decision health.

Examples include:

- Average decision cycle time.
- Escalation frequency.
- Decision backlog.
- Issue aging.
- Executive response times.
- Rework resulting from delayed decisions.

These measures provide visibility.

They help organizations identify bottlenecks.

They reveal where execution may be slowing.

Decision health often predicts execution health.

The AVA Perspective

Within the AVA Enterprise Value Realization System, decision velocity influences every pillar.

AVA Assess™ evaluates whether decision capacity exists.

AVA Execute™ depends upon timely decisions.

AVA Tech™ requires technology decisions.

AVA Exit™ depends upon transition decisions.

AVA Assure™ evaluates the impact of decision delays.

AVA Intelligence™ increasingly helps identify decision risks before they become problems.

Decision velocity spans the entire lifecycle of value realization.

Speed Matters

Organizations often ask:

"Did we make the right decision?"

A second question may be equally important:

"Did we make the decision soon enough?"

Because delayed decisions frequently reduce options.

Increase costs.

Create risks.

And destroy value.

The future belongs to organizations that can make informed decisions quickly.

Organizations that combine:

- Leadership.
- Accountability.
- Governance.
- Information.
- Courage.

Decision velocity is not simply an operational capability.

It is a competitive advantage.

Because organizations do not execute at the speed of their plans.

They do not execute at the speed of their technology.

They do not execute at the speed of their budgets.

Organizations execute at the speed of their decisions.

And in modern business, speed often determines who realizes value and who loses it.

Chapter 16 - Building an Execution-First Culture

"Strategy may define the destination, but culture determines whether the organization ever arrives."

Every organization has a strategy.

Most have governance structures.

Many have project management methodologies, performance dashboards, executive steering committees, and transformation offices.

Yet despite all of these investments, organizations continue to struggle to execute consistently.

The difference is rarely intelligence.

It is rarely effort.

It is almost never the strategy itself.

The difference is culture.

Culture determines how quickly organizations make decisions, how they respond to uncertainty, how they manage accountability, and whether execution becomes everyone's responsibility or no one's responsibility.

An organization can hire experienced executives, implement sophisticated technology, and develop comprehensive integration plans. None of those investments will consistently create enterprise value if the culture does not reinforce execution.

Execution is not an event.

Execution is a way of operating.

Organizations that consistently outperform their competitors do not simply execute individual projects well. They build cultures where disciplined execution becomes part of everyday decision-making. They institutionalize the behaviors, expectations, and leadership practices that enable people to transform strategic intent into measurable business outcomes.

That is what an execution-first culture looks like.

Culture Is the Invisible Operating System

Culture is often described as "the way we do things around here."

While simple, that definition captures an important truth.

Culture influences thousands of decisions every day.

It determines whether problems are escalated early or hidden until they become crises.

It determines whether teams collaborate across functions or optimize for their own departments.

It determines whether executives make timely decisions or postpone difficult conversations.

It determines whether accountability is embraced or avoided.

Most importantly, culture determines whether execution receives the same level of attention as strategy.

Organizations rarely fail because they lack intelligent people.

They fail because their culture unintentionally rewards planning more than delivery.

Meetings celebrate presentations instead of outcomes.

Leaders reward activity instead of value creation.

Teams protect functional objectives instead of enterprise objectives.

These behaviors create value leakage long before financial results begin to decline.

Leadership Creates Culture

Execution-first cultures never emerge by accident.

They are created by leadership.

Employees observe what leaders prioritize, what they measure, how they make decisions, and what behaviors they consistently reward.

If executives repeatedly delay decisions, others learn that delay is acceptable.

If leaders tolerate missed commitments without accountability, execution discipline begins to deteriorate.

Conversely, when leaders demonstrate urgency, transparency, ownership, and accountability, those behaviors spread throughout the organization.

Culture follows leadership.

This is why execution must become an executive responsibility rather than a project management responsibility.

The tone established by leadership ultimately determines the execution capability of the enterprise.

Accountability Is a Cultural Choice

Many organizations believe they have accountability because responsibilities are documented within organizational charts.

Real accountability is different.

Accountability means every individual understands how their decisions contribute to enterprise value.

It means commitments are visible.

Progress is transparent.

Problems are surfaced early.

Corrective actions are expected.

In execution-first cultures, accountability is viewed as a source of empowerment rather than punishment.

People understand expectations.

They receive timely feedback.

They are encouraged to solve problems before they become organizational risks.

This creates confidence instead of fear.

Collaboration Creates Enterprise Value

Enterprise transformations cannot succeed when departments optimize independently.

Finance cannot realize value without Operations.

Operations cannot execute without Technology.

Technology cannot deliver without Human Resources.

Every function depends on another.

Execution-first cultures recognize these interdependencies.

Success is measured by enterprise outcomes rather than departmental achievements.

Leaders actively remove organizational silos, encourage cross-functional collaboration, and reinforce shared accountability for value realization.

The objective is no longer successful projects.

The objective is successful enterprises.

Learning Organizations Execute Better

No transformation unfolds exactly as planned.

Unexpected risks emerge.

Priorities shift.

Assumptions change.

Execution-first cultures do not resist change.

They learn from it.

Every Value Assurance Review, governance meeting, post-implementation review, and benefits realization assessment becomes an opportunity to improve future execution.

Lessons learned are documented.

Processes evolve.

Capabilities mature.

Execution becomes increasingly repeatable.

Continuous learning transforms execution from individual expertise into organizational capability.

Measuring Execution Culture

Culture should not remain an abstract concept.

It can be observed.

It can be measured.

Indicators of an execution-first culture include:

- Decision velocity
- Accountability completion rates
- Cross-functional collaboration
- Escalation responsiveness
- Governance effectiveness
- Risk resolution
- Benefits realization performance
- Employee engagement during transformation
- Stakeholder confidence
- Continuous improvement adoption

These indicators reveal whether execution has become embedded within the organization or remains dependent upon individual leaders.

Building an Execution-First Enterprise

Execution-first cultures are built intentionally.

They begin with leadership commitment.

They mature through governance.

They are reinforced through accountability.

They improve through continuous learning.

They are sustained through Value Assurance.

This is where the five pillars of Enterprise Value Realization converge.

AVA Assess™ establishes readiness.

AVA Execute™ provides disciplined delivery.

AVA Lead™ creates executive alignment and leadership.

AVA Tech™ enables the organization through technology.

AVA Exit™ ensures sustainable transition.

AVA Assure™ continuously evaluates and strengthens execution across every phase of the Value Realization Lifecycle.

Together, these capabilities create organizations that consistently transform strategy into measurable enterprise value.

Culture Determines Value

Organizations often ask how they can execute better.

The better question is whether their culture enables execution.

Processes can be copied.

Technology can be purchased.

Frameworks can be adopted.

Culture must be built.

Organizations that make execution part of their identity consistently outperform those that view execution as a temporary initiative.

The future belongs to organizations that develop execution as a core organizational capability.

Because when execution becomes culture, value realization becomes predictable.

And when value realization becomes predictable, enterprise performance becomes sustainable.

PART V - VALUE ASSURANCE

Organizations often devote tremendous attention to planning, execution, and delivery, yet surprisingly little attention to determining whether the value they intended to create is actually being realized. Projects may finish on schedule. Integrations may achieve Day One readiness. Technology systems may be deployed. Transformation programs may complete their planned activities. Yet months or years later, leaders frequently discover that expected benefits have diminished, organizational alignment has weakened, and enterprise value has slowly eroded.

Value realization is not a single milestone achieved at the conclusion of a program. It is an ongoing discipline that requires continuous oversight, independent assessment, leadership engagement, and a willingness to confront uncomfortable realities before value is lost. Organizations that consistently realize value understand that measurement, accountability, and assurance must continue long after the initial excitement of a transaction or transformation has passed.

The AVA Enterprise Value Realization System recognizes that value must be protected across all five pillars. AVA Assess™ confirms that organizations understand their risks and readiness. AVA Execute™ monitors delivery and accountability. AVA Lead™ evaluates leadership alignment, communication, and organizational effectiveness. AVA Tech™ ensures that technology continues to enable the business. AVA Exit™ focuses on sustainability, transition, and long-term operational success.

Supporting these pillars are two enterprise-wide capabilities that increasingly define modern value realization. AVA Intelligence™ provides predictive insights, emerging risk identification, trend analysis, and decision support that help organizations recognize issues before they become visible. AVA Assure™ provides independent value assurance reviews, benefits realization assessments, governance evaluations, and executive oversight designed to protect enterprise value throughout the lifecycle.

Yet value assurance extends beyond metrics, dashboards, and reviews. It requires leaders who ask difficult questions, organizations willing to challenge assumptions, and experienced professionals who share the lessons they have learned with others. Many of the failures that organizations encounter have been experienced before. The responsibility of today's leaders is not only to protect value for their organizations, but also to transfer knowledge, mentor future leaders, and preserve the experiences that can help others succeed.

The chapters in this section explore how organizations can move beyond measuring activity and begin measuring outcomes. They examine the disciplines required to verify benefits realization, identify value leakage, provide independent assurance, and sustain enterprise value over time. Ultimately, value assurance is not simply about determining whether work was completed. It is about ensuring that the value promised at the beginning of the journey is ultimately realized and that the knowledge gained along the way is passed to those who will lead the next generation of transformations.

Chapter 17 - AVA Assure™

Protecting Enterprise Value

"What gets measured gets managed. What gets assured gets realized."

Value Is Not Lost Overnight

One of the greatest misconceptions in enterprise transformation is the belief that value disappears at a single point in time.

It rarely does.

Enterprise value is almost never destroyed by one catastrophic decision or one failed milestone. More often, it erodes gradually through hundreds of small decisions, unresolved dependencies, delayed actions, unmanaged risks, and assumptions that quietly go unchallenged. A missed milestone becomes an accepted delay. A deferred decision extends beyond the next steering committee meeting. A business process remains undefined. Technology readiness slips. Stakeholder engagement declines. Benefits that once appeared certain slowly become increasingly difficult to achieve.

Each event appears manageable in isolation.

Collectively, they become value leakage.

By the time financial performance reflects the problem, the opportunity to prevent it has often passed.

The organizations that consistently realize value understand this reality. They do not wait for quarterly financial results or post-implementation reviews to determine whether execution is succeeding. They continuously evaluate execution health, organizational readiness, emerging risks, decision quality, and progress toward business outcomes throughout the lifecycle of every significant initiative.

This continuous discipline is the purpose of AVA Assure™.

Assurance Is Not Auditing

Traditional assurance functions frequently focus on compliance.

Did the organization follow the required process?

Were approvals obtained?

Were governance requirements satisfied?

Were controls documented?

These are important questions, but they do not answer the question executives ultimately care about.

Are we still on track to realize the value we promised?

AVA Assure™ shifts the focus from compliance to confidence.

It asks whether execution remains aligned with enterprise objectives, whether assumptions continue to be valid, whether benefits remain achievable, and whether leadership has sufficient insight to make timely decisions.

The objective is not to evaluate yesterday's performance.

It is to improve tomorrow's decisions.

Assurance Across the Enterprise Value Realization Lifecycle

AVA Assure™ is not a phase of execution.

It is a continuous capability that spans every stage of enterprise value realization.

During opportunity framing, assurance validates whether the value hypothesis is realistic and whether critical assumptions have been tested.

During due diligence and planning, it evaluates organizational readiness, technology maturity, governance structures, resource capacity, and execution risk before commitments become irreversible.

Throughout execution, it continually monitors progress, identifies value leakage, evaluates dependency health, and confirms that benefits remain achievable.

As initiatives mature, assurance validates operational readiness, organizational adoption, capability maturity, and benefit realization.

Finally, after implementation, AVA Assure™ confirms that enterprise value has been sustained rather than temporarily achieved.

At every stage, the objective remains the same.

Protect enterprise value before it is lost.

The Five Dimensions of Enterprise Assurance

AVA Assure™ evaluates organizations through five integrated dimensions.

Strategic Assurance

Does execution remain aligned with the organization's strategic objectives?

Have business priorities changed?

Do expected outcomes continue to justify the investment?

Has the original value hypothesis remained valid?

Execution Assurance

Is the initiative executing effectively?

Are milestones meaningful?

Are dependencies actively managed?

Are decisions being made with sufficient speed?

Is accountability clear?

Organizational Assurance

Are people prepared for the change?

Are leaders aligned?

Is adoption progressing?

Does the organization possess sufficient execution capacity to absorb the transformation?

Technology Assurance

Does technology enable rather than constrain value realization?

Are critical systems ready?

Are data migration activities progressing appropriately?

Do cybersecurity, infrastructure, integration, and application readiness support operational success?

Value Assurance

Most importantly:

Is the enterprise still positioned to achieve the financial, operational, strategic, and cultural outcomes that justified the investment?

Everything ultimately returns to this question.

Detecting Value Leakage Early

AVA Assure™ emphasizes leading indicators rather than waiting for lagging results.

Financial performance is an outcome.

Execution behavior is the predictor.

Examples of leading indicators include:

- Increasing decision latency
- Declining executive engagement
- Growing dependency risk
- Technology readiness deterioration
- Stakeholder resistance
- Resource overload
- Benefit realization delays
- Organizational fatigue
- Scope instability
- Governance inconsistency

Individually, each indicator may appear manageable.

Together, they often provide an early warning that enterprise value is beginning to erode.

AVA Assure™ is designed to identify these signals while corrective action remains possible.

Confidence Rather Than Status

Traditional reporting frequently categorizes initiatives using simple status indicators.

Green.

Yellow.

Red.

These indicators describe activity.

They rarely describe confidence.

AVA Assure™ instead asks a more meaningful question:

How confident should leadership be that the expected enterprise value will ultimately be realized?

Confidence reflects far more than schedule performance.

It considers leadership alignment, execution quality, organizational readiness, technology maturity, dependency health, governance effectiveness, benefit realization, operational preparedness, and emerging risk.

This provides executives with a far richer understanding of enterprise performance than traditional status reporting.

Executive Decision Support

The purpose of assurance is not to generate reports.

It is to improve decisions.

Effective assurance enables executives to understand:

Where value is being created.

Where value is at risk.

Which assumptions require validation.

Which decisions require immediate attention.

Which dependencies threaten future success.

Where organizational capacity is becoming constrained.

Which corrective actions will have the greatest impact.

In this way, AVA Assure™ becomes an executive decision support capability rather than simply a governance process.

The Foundation for Enterprise Intelligence

As organizations increasingly integrate operational, financial, project, and technology data, assurance evolves beyond periodic reviews.

The future of enterprise assurance lies in continuous enterprise intelligence.

Rather than waiting for scheduled governance meetings, organizations will increasingly use connected data, structured knowledge, predictive analytics, and intelligent decision support to continuously evaluate execution health and enterprise value realization.

AVA Assure™ establishes the methodology for that future.

It defines what should be measured, why it matters, and how leaders should respond.

The technology that enables continuous intelligence will evolve.

The underlying principles of enterprise assurance will remain constant.

Protecting What Matters Most

Every organization invests in the future.

Some invest through acquisitions.

Others through technology.

Others through innovation, operational excellence, capital projects, or organizational transformation.

Regardless of the initiative, the objective is always the same.

Create more value tomorrow than exists today.

AVA Assure™ exists to ensure that objective remains visible throughout the journey.

Not by replacing leadership.

Not by increasing bureaucracy.

Not by adding another governance layer.

But by providing continuous confidence that execution remains aligned with enterprise value.

Because organizations do not lose value when a project slips.

They lose value when no one recognizes what that slip means.

Protecting enterprise value begins long before financial results reveal a problem.

It begins with continuously understanding whether the organization is still on the path to realizing the value it set out to create.

That is the purpose of AVA Assure™.

And that is why protecting enterprise value is ultimately a leadership responsibility rather than a reporting exercise.

Chapter 18 - Benefits Realization

Organizations do not pursue mergers, acquisitions, divestitures, technology implementations, or major transformations simply to complete projects.

They pursue them to create value.

The transaction closes to create growth.

The integration occurs to generate synergies.

The technology investment promises improvements.

The transformation seeks better performance.

The objective is never the activity itself.

The objective is the benefit.

Yet many organizations treat benefits realization as the final phase of execution.

In reality, benefits realization is the purpose of execution.

Every chapter in this book ultimately leads to a single question:

Did the organization realize the value it expected?

The Difference Between Outputs and Outcomes

Projects produce outputs.

Systems go live.

Organizations restructure.

Processes change.

Teams complete activities.

Milestones are achieved.

These outputs are important.

However, outputs do not automatically create value.

Benefits represent outcomes.

Reduced costs.

Improved performance.

Increased revenue.

Higher productivity.

Better decision making.

Improved customer experiences.

Greater organizational capability.

The distinction matters.

Organizations frequently celebrate outputs while failing to measure outcomes.

The implementation succeeds.

The value does not.

The Benefits Gap

Many organizations experience a gap between expected benefits and realized benefits.

The business case projected savings.

The acquisition model estimated synergies.

The transformation promised improvements.

Months later, the expected results fail to appear.

This gap emerges for many reasons:

- Leadership attention shifts.
- Benefits lack ownership.
- Measurements are unclear.
- Assumptions change.
- Risks materialize.
- Priorities compete.
- Accountability disappears.

The benefits gap represents one of the largest sources of value leakage.

Organizations complete the work.

But they fail to realize the value.

Ownership Determines Outcomes

One of the simplest questions often produces the most difficult answer.

Who owns the benefit?

Organizations frequently assign ownership for:

- Schedules.

- Budgets.
- Risks.
- Activities.

Benefits frequently belong to everyone.

Or no one.

Benefits realization requires ownership.

Every significant benefit should have:

- An owner.
- A measurement.
- A target.
- A timeline.
- Accountability.

Ownership creates focus.

Focus improves outcomes.

Benefits that have owners are far more likely to be realized.

Measuring Benefits

Organizations cannot improve what they do not measure.

Benefits measurement often includes:

Financial Benefits

- Cost reductions.
- Synergies.
- Revenue growth.
- Margin improvements.
- Cash flow improvements.

Operational Benefits

- Productivity improvements.
- Process efficiencies.
- Cycle time reductions.
- Service improvements.

Organizational Benefits

- Leadership effectiveness.
- Decision quality.
- Employee engagement.
- Capability development.

Strategic Benefits

- Market growth.
- Competitive advantages.
- Technology capabilities.
- Future opportunities.

The most successful organizations measure benefits continuously.

Not simply at the end.

Benefits Have Life Cycles

Benefits rarely appear immediately.

Many organizations expect value to materialize shortly after implementation.

The reality is often more complex.

Some benefits emerge quickly.

Others require:

- Organizational adoption.
- Process maturity.
- Technology stabilization.
- Behavioral changes.
- Operational improvements.

Benefits frequently follow a curve.

Initial disruption.

Stabilization.

Improvement.

Optimization.

Organizations that understand this pattern establish realistic expectations.

They continue measuring after implementation concludes.

Sustaining Benefits

Realizing value is difficult.

Sustaining value may be even more difficult.

Organizations frequently achieve improvements only to see them disappear.

Processes revert.

Behaviors return.

Leadership changes.

Priorities shift.

Performance declines.

Sustainability requires:

- Accountability.
- Leadership.
- Measurement.
- Governance.
- Ownership.

Benefits must become part of the operating model.

Not simply part of the project.

The Business Owns the Benefits

Project teams facilitate change.

Integration teams coordinate execution.

Technology teams enable solutions.

Ultimately, the business owns the benefits.

Once execution concludes:

- Operations must sustain performance.
- Leaders must maintain accountability.
- Organizations must continue measuring outcomes.

Benefits realization cannot remain with temporary teams.

It must transfer to permanent ownership.

This transition often determines whether value survives.

The Role of Leadership

Leadership remains essential throughout benefits realization.

Executives establish expectations.

Allocate resources.

Review performance.

Reinforce accountability.

Organizations frequently lose momentum when leadership attention moves elsewhere.

Benefits become assumptions.

Measurements stop.

Ownership weakens.

Value begins to leak.

Leaders who continue asking:

"Are we realizing the expected value?"

often achieve better outcomes.

Leadership attention protects benefits.

Benefits Realization and AVA Assure™

AVA Assure™ exists to support benefits realization.

It provides:

- Visibility.
- Measurement.
- Accountability.

- Early warning indicators.
- Leadership insight.

Benefits realization does not occur automatically.

Organizations require:

- Continuous monitoring.
- Value assurance reviews.
- Benefit ownership.
- Performance measurement.

AVA Assure™ helps organizations maintain focus on outcomes.

Because the objective is not merely completing the work.

The objective is realizing the value.

The Future of Benefits Realization

Organizations increasingly recognize that benefits should be managed with the same discipline as financial performance.

Future capabilities may include:

- Real-time dashboards.
- Benefit scorecards.
- Predictive analytics.
- Artificial intelligence.
- Automated reporting.
- Leading indicators.

These capabilities improve visibility.

They strengthen accountability.

They support decisions.

Benefits realization will increasingly become an enterprise discipline.

The Final Measure of Success

Organizations frequently ask:

- Was the project successful?
- Did the integration finish?
- Did the system go live?
- Did the transition occur?

These questions matter.

But they are not the ultimate measure.

The final measure is value.

Did costs decline?

Did revenues improve?

Did performance increase?

Did capabilities strengthen?

Did the organization achieve what it set out to accomplish?

Benefits realization answers these questions.

It connects strategy to outcomes.

Execution to value.

Leadership to performance.

Because organizations do not pursue change simply to complete activities.

They pursue change to create better outcomes.

Projects end.

Programs conclude.

Teams disband.

Benefits remain.

And the ultimate purpose of execution is not to deliver work.

It is to deliver value.

Because in the end, value is not realized when the transaction closes.

Value is not realized when the implementation finishes.

Value is realized when the expected benefits become measurable, sustainable, and real.

That is the true measure of success.

That is the purpose of enterprise value realization.

Chapter 19 - The Rise of AVA Intelligence™

"The future of execution will not be determined by artificial intelligence alone. It will be determined by how intelligently organizations apply it."

Every generation of business experiences a technology that fundamentally changes how organizations operate.

Mainframe computing transformed financial management.

Enterprise Resource Planning systems integrated business operations.

Cloud computing redefined scalability.

Digital transformation connected organizations in ways previously unimaginable.

Artificial Intelligence represents the next transformation.

But unlike previous technologies, AI is not simply another business application.

It is becoming an enterprise capability.

For organizations managing mergers, acquisitions, divestitures, and enterprise transformations, AI offers something the industry has never truly possessed before:

The ability to continuously observe, analyze, predict, and improve execution while work is still in progress.

This is where AVA Intelligence™ begins.

Beyond Artificial Intelligence

Much of today's conversation focuses on using AI to generate reports, summarize meetings, write documents, or answer questions.

These capabilities are valuable.

But they barely scratch the surface of AI's potential.

The greatest opportunity is not document generation.

The greatest opportunity is enterprise intelligence.

Imagine an organization where every governance meeting, project update, risk register, benefits dashboard, decision log, dependency tracker, financial forecast, and technology roadmap continuously contributes to a living understanding of execution health.

Instead of waiting for monthly reports, executives receive real-time insight.

Instead of discovering problems after value has already been lost, leaders identify emerging risks while corrective action is still possible.

Instead of asking what happened, organizations understand what is happening—and what is likely to happen next.

That is enterprise intelligence.

Introducing AVA Intelligence™

AVA Intelligence™ is the enterprise intelligence layer of the AVA Enterprise Value Realization System.

It does not replace executive judgment.

It strengthens it.

It does not replace governance.

It makes governance smarter.

It does not replace leadership.

It provides leaders with clearer visibility, faster insight, and better information.

AVA Intelligence™ continuously evaluates execution across the entire Value Realization Lifecycle.

It brings together structured data, operational metrics, governance information, project health, technology readiness, financial performance, organizational indicators, and Value Assurance Reviews to create a comprehensive understanding of enterprise execution.

Its purpose is simple:

Provide executives with the intelligence required to protect and realize enterprise value.

From Data to Decisions

Organizations possess enormous amounts of information.

Most possess very little intelligence.

Spreadsheets, dashboards, project plans, issue logs, financial reports, meeting minutes, and risk registers all contain valuable information.

Unfortunately, these assets often exist in isolation.

Executives are expected to combine hundreds of disconnected data points into coherent decisions.

AVA Intelligence™ changes this dynamic.

It connects information across the enterprise.

Patterns become visible.

Dependencies become apparent.

Emerging risks become measurable.

Decision-making becomes proactive instead of reactive.

Information becomes intelligence.

Continuous Organizational Health

Traditional governance relies upon periodic reporting.

Monthly steering committee meetings.

Quarterly business reviews.

Scheduled Value Assurance Reviews.

These remain important.

But AI enables something fundamentally different.

Continuous assessment.

Instead of reviewing organizational health every thirty days, AVA Intelligence™ continuously evaluates execution performance.

It monitors leading indicators.

It analyzes trends.

It identifies anomalies.

It highlights deteriorating conditions before they become executive crises.

Organizations move from periodic awareness to continuous awareness.

Predicting Value Leakage

One of the greatest challenges in enterprise execution is identifying value leakage before financial performance begins to decline.

By the time expected synergies disappear from financial statements, recovery is often difficult.

AVA Intelligence™ seeks earlier signals.

Delayed decisions.

Increasing issue resolution times.

Growing dependency backlogs.

Technology implementation delays.

Resource constraints.

Declining stakeholder engagement.

Governance bottlenecks.

Each indicator may appear insignificant independently.

Together, they reveal emerging execution risk.

This allows organizations to intervene while value can still be protected.

Executive Decision Support

Leadership has never suffered from a lack of information.

Leadership suffers from a lack of clarity.

AVA Intelligence™ provides executives with prioritized insights rather than overwhelming volumes of data.

Instead of asking leaders to review hundreds of reports, the system identifies the few issues requiring immediate attention.

Decision support becomes focused.

Executive conversations become more strategic.

Governance meetings become shorter, more productive, and more action-oriented.

Decision velocity increases.

Execution improves.

Enhancing the Five Pillars

AVA Intelligence™ strengthens every pillar of the AVA Enterprise Value Realization System.

AVA Assess™

AI evaluates execution readiness, organizational maturity, historical performance, and emerging risks before execution begins.

AVA Execute™™

Execution plans, dependencies, milestones, and delivery performance are continuously monitored for emerging issues.

AVA Lead™

Leadership receives actionable insights that improve governance, decision-making, executive alignment, and organizational communication.

AVA Tech™™

Technology readiness, cybersecurity exposure, application integration, data migration, and digital transformation initiatives become continuously visible.

AVA Exit™

Transition readiness, TSA dependencies, operational independence, and sustainability indicators are monitored throughout transition execution.

Across every pillar, AVA Intelligence™ provides greater visibility, faster insight, and earlier intervention.

Enhancing AVA Assure™

AVA Assure™ remains the discipline responsible for independently evaluating enterprise execution.

AVA Intelligence™ dramatically strengthens that discipline.

Rather than relying solely on scheduled reviews, AI continuously evaluates organizational health between assessments.

Value Assurance Reviews become richer.

Recommendations become more targeted.

Corrective actions become more timely.

Benefits realization becomes more predictable.

Human expertise and artificial intelligence reinforce one another.

The Human Advantage

Artificial Intelligence will never replace executive leadership.

It cannot establish organizational trust.

It cannot negotiate competing priorities.

It cannot inspire teams during uncertainty.

It cannot exercise wisdom developed through decades of experience.

Leadership remains fundamentally human.

AVA Intelligence™ exists to make leaders better.

The organizations that achieve the greatest success will not replace experienced leaders with AI.

They will combine experienced leaders with intelligent systems.

This partnership creates capabilities neither could achieve independently.

The Next Evolution of Enterprise Execution

Every generation develops better execution tools.

Project management software improved planning.

Enterprise systems improved coordination.

Digital platforms improved collaboration.

Artificial Intelligence improves understanding.

The next generation of organizations will not simply manage execution.

They will continuously learn from it.

They will identify risks before they become failures.

They will improve governance while work is still in progress.

They will measure benefits continuously rather than retrospectively.

Most importantly, they will transform enterprise execution from a reactive discipline into a continuously improving organizational capability.

That is the promise of AVA Intelligence™.

It is not merely another technology.

It is the intelligence layer that enables organizations to consistently transform strategy into sustainable enterprise value.

And it represents the next chapter in the evolution of Enterprise Value Realization.

PART VI - THE FUTURE OF EXECUTION

The future of business will not be defined solely by strategy, technology, capital, or scale. Increasingly, organizations will compete based upon their ability to execute, adapt, and consistently realize value.

Business environments continue to accelerate. Technology evolves more rapidly. Organizational complexity increases. Decision cycles shorten. Artificial intelligence, data analytics, automation, and digital transformation are reshaping how organizations operate and how leaders make decisions. At the same time, stakeholders expect organizations to deliver results more quickly, manage greater levels of risk, and sustain value long after implementation activities have concluded.

These changes are transforming execution itself.

Organizations can no longer rely solely on experience, intuition, or traditional management approaches. They require greater visibility, better information, stronger leadership, and more intelligent ways of understanding the conditions that influence value realization. The future of execution will increasingly depend upon an organization's ability to identify risks earlier, recognize patterns sooner, improve decision making, and continuously protect enterprise value.

The chapters in this section explore the emergence of AVA Intelligence™ as an enterprise-wide capability, the rise of the Value Realization Enterprise, and the growing recognition that execution itself has become a strategic advantage. AVA Intelligence™ spans the entire AVA Enterprise Value Realization System, providing insight, visibility, and increasingly predictive capabilities that support leadership and strengthen outcomes. The Value Realization Enterprise represents a new organizational model—one that intentionally develops the capabilities required to repeatedly transform strategy into measurable results.

The organizations that succeed in the future will not simply manage projects more effectively.

They will build execution capabilities into the enterprise itself.

They will understand readiness before action.

They will protect value throughout execution.

They will leverage technology to enable performance.

They will sustain benefits beyond implementation.

And they will increasingly use intelligence to improve decisions before value is lost.

Because the future belongs to organizations that do more than develop strategy.

The future belongs to organizations that consistently realize value.

Chapter 20 - The Rise of the Value Realization Enterprise

Every generation of business leaders faces a defining challenge.

Previous generations focused on industrial efficiency, quality improvement, globalization, supply chain optimization, lean manufacturing, and digital transformation. Each era developed its own management philosophies, operating models, and leadership disciplines that shaped the organizations of the future.

The next defining challenge is enterprise value realization.

Organizations today possess extraordinary strategic capabilities. They conduct sophisticated analyses, develop complex business cases, leverage advanced technologies, and pursue increasingly ambitious transformations. Yet despite these capabilities, many organizations continue to struggle with the same fundamental problem:

They fail to consistently realize the value they intended to create.

The future will belong to organizations that move beyond managing projects, transactions, and individual initiatives and begin managing enterprise value itself.

These organizations will become Value Realization Enterprises.

A Value Realization Enterprise understands that value is not created by strategy alone. It recognizes that value emerges through a disciplined system that aligns leadership, execution, technology, organizational readiness, and long-term sustainability.

This system is represented by the AVA Enterprise Value Realization System.

AVA Assess™ ensures that organizations understand opportunity, readiness, risk, and complexity before significant commitments are made.

AVA Execute™™ provides the governance, accountability, decision-making, and operational discipline required to deliver results.

AVA Lead™ aligns leaders, develops organizations, and guides people through change.

AVA Tech™™ enables value through technology, cybersecurity, data, and digital capabilities.

AVA Exit™ ensures that value remains sustainable through transition, ownership, and operational stability.

Organizations that strengthen all five pillars create conditions that allow value to be realized consistently rather than accidentally.

However, the future of value realization will require more than these foundational disciplines.

Organizations increasingly operate in environments characterized by rapid change, growing complexity, expanding technology ecosystems, and unprecedented amounts of information. Leaders are expected to make faster decisions while managing greater uncertainty.

Information alone is no longer sufficient.

The future requires intelligence.

AVA Intelligence™ represents the next evolution of enterprise execution. Artificial intelligence, predictive analytics, early warning indicators, decision support, and pattern recognition will increasingly help organizations identify emerging risks, understand dependencies, forecast outcomes, and protect enterprise value before problems become visible.

Organizations will increasingly ask:

- Where is value at risk?

- What decisions are slowing progress?
- Which benefits may not be realized?
- Where are dependencies increasing?
- What risks are emerging?

The organizations that answer these questions earliest will possess significant advantages.

At the same time, future organizations must recognize that measurement alone does not guarantee success.

Value must be continuously validated.

AVA Assure™ represents the growing importance of independent oversight, value assurance, benefits realization, governance assessments, and executive reviews. Organizations can no longer wait until the end of a program to determine whether value was achieved.

They must continuously ask:

Are we realizing the value we intended to create?

The Value Realization Enterprise measures not simply activity, but outcomes.

It measures not only schedules, but benefits.

It measures not only completion, but sustainability.

It measures not only delivery, but value.

Yet perhaps the most important characteristic of the Value Realization Enterprise has little to do with processes, governance models, or technology.

It has to do with people.

The future will require leaders who can integrate business strategy, execution, technology, organizational change, and value realization into a unified discipline. These leaders must possess technical capability, business judgment, emotional intelligence, and the ability to guide organizations through uncertainty.

They must become teachers as well as leaders.

Throughout history, organizations have depended upon experienced professionals to pass knowledge to those who follow them. Much of the knowledge that drives successful execution has traditionally been transferred through mentoring, coaching, observation, and experience.

Today, many organizations face the loss of institutional knowledge as experienced leaders retire and fewer opportunities exist for direct mentoring and development.

The Value Realization Enterprise recognizes that knowledge itself is an enterprise asset.

Experienced leaders become mentors.

Program leaders become teachers.

Executives become coaches.

Organizations intentionally develop future leaders.

Lessons learned become lessons shared.

The transfer of knowledge becomes a strategic responsibility.

Legacy becomes part of value realization.

Future leaders will inherit increasingly complex organizations, more advanced technologies, greater stakeholder expectations, and faster rates of change. They will need more than methodologies and tools.

They will need judgment.

They will need perspective.

They will need guidance.

They will need the experiences of those who came before them.

The organizations that thrive in the future will not simply build stronger processes. They will build stronger leaders.

They will invest in mentoring.

They will preserve institutional knowledge.

They will encourage teaching.

They will reward leadership development.

They will recognize that the next generation of value realization depends upon the next generation of leaders.

The rise of the Value Realization Enterprise is not simply the emergence of a new management framework.

It is the recognition that organizations must intentionally connect readiness, execution, leadership, technology, transition, intelligence, assurance, and human development into a single enterprise system.

The future will belong to organizations that:

Assess honestly.

Execute consistently.

Lead courageously.

Enable through technology.

Transition successfully.

Apply intelligence.

Provide assurance.

Develop people.

Share knowledge.

Build legacy.

Because ultimately, the organizations that create the greatest value will be those that not only realize value for today, but prepare others to realize value tomorrow.

That is the future of enterprise value realization.

That is the rise of the Value Realization Enterprise.

Chapter 21 - Execution Determines Value

The Future Belongs to the Enterprise That Can Execute

Throughout this book, we have examined why organizations lose value after mergers and acquisitions, why strategic initiatives fail to deliver their intended outcomes, and why so many transformations consume extraordinary amounts of time, money, and human effort without achieving the business value that justified the investment.

Although the examples have often been drawn from mergers and acquisitions, the lessons extend far beyond a single discipline. Every organization undertakes initiatives designed to improve its future. Whether implementing new technology, entering a new market, restructuring operations, modernizing infrastructure, integrating an acquisition, or launching an enterprise-wide transformation, the objective is always the same: create more value tomorrow than exists today.

The uncomfortable reality is that value is rarely lost because organizations lack ambition, intelligence, or strategic vision. It is lost because execution is inconsistent, fragmented, reactive, and disconnected from the outcomes it was intended to achieve.

Strategy creates opportunity.

Execution determines whether opportunity becomes value.

That principle applies equally to the boardroom, the executive suite, the program office, the project team, and every employee responsible for transforming vision into reality.

For decades, organizations have invested heavily in improving strategy development, financial planning, operational efficiency, technology, and governance. Each discipline has matured into its own profession with established standards, methodologies, and certifications. Yet one critical capability has remained surprisingly underdeveloped—the ability to consistently convert enterprise investment into realized business value.

Execution has too often been viewed as the responsibility of project managers rather than executive leaders. Projects have been measured by schedule, budget, and scope while executives measured financial performance months or years later. Somewhere between those two perspectives, enterprise value disappeared.

That gap is where value leakage occurs.

The organizations that will lead the next generation of business will close that gap.

They will no longer separate strategy from execution or execution from value realization. Instead, they will recognize that these are inseparable components of a single enterprise discipline.

Execution will become an organizational capability rather than an individual skill.

Governance will become a mechanism for accelerating decisions rather than controlling activity.

Technology will become an enabler of enterprise intelligence rather than simply a collection of applications.

Leadership will be measured not only by the strategies conceived but by the value consistently realized.

This is the foundation of the Value Realization Enterprise.

It is an organization that continuously aligns strategy, execution, technology, governance, and leadership around one objective: realizing measurable enterprise value.

This is why the AVA Enterprise Value Realization System extends beyond traditional project management or mergers and acquisitions. Its principles apply wherever organizations invest resources in pursuit of better outcomes. Whether guiding a billion-dollar acquisition, an ERP implementation, a digital transformation, a capital program, or a strategic growth initiative, the same question ultimately defines success:

Did the organization realize the value it intended to create?

The five pillars of AVA—Assess, Execute, Lead, Tech, and Exit—provide the operational disciplines necessary to answer that question. AVA Assure™ spans those pillars, continuously validating progress, identifying emerging risks, and ensuring that execution remains aligned with enterprise objectives. AVA Intelligence™ represents the future evolution of that philosophy: using structured enterprise knowledge, connected data, predictive analytics, and intelligent decision support to provide leaders with continuous visibility into execution health and value realization.

The goal is not to replace executive judgment.

The goal is to enhance it.

Imagine an executive team that no longer waits for monthly reports to discover problems. Imagine a board of directors that understands not only what has happened, but what is likely to happen next. Imagine a steering committee that can immediately see how a delayed decision affects technology readiness, operational capability, financial benefits, and shareholder value. Imagine an organization where every strategic initiative can be evaluated at any moment against a single question:

Are we still on track to realize the value we promised?

That is the future of enterprise execution.

It is also the future of enterprise leadership.

The leaders of tomorrow will not simply make better decisions because they possess more information. They will make better decisions because they possess better understanding. They will see relationships instead of isolated metrics. They will recognize leading indicators before they become failures. They will understand that value is created through thousands of interconnected decisions executed consistently over time.

Organizations that develop this capability will not merely complete projects more effectively.

They will become organizations designed to realize value continuously.

As I reflect on more than three decades of leading projects, programs, mergers, acquisitions, divestitures, and enterprise transformations, one lesson stands above all others.

Successful organizations are not defined by the strategies they announce, the technologies they purchase, or the transactions they complete.

They are defined by their ability to execute.

That ability is not accidental.

It can be designed.

It can be measured.

It can be strengthened.

It can become part of an organization's culture.

And when it does, execution ceases to be a competitive advantage.

It becomes the organization's identity.

The future will belong to organizations that understand this simple truth.

Not because they pursue more opportunities.

Not because they invest more capital.

Not because they employ more sophisticated technology.

But because they have built the institutional capability to transform vision into measurable, sustainable enterprise value.

That is the purpose of enterprise execution.

That is the purpose of value realization.

That is the future of leadership.

And ultimately, that is why one principle rises above all others:

Execution determines value.

Conclusion - The Journey to Value Begins with Execution

When I began my career more than thirty years ago, I believed that success was primarily the result of good planning, experienced leadership, and disciplined project management. Those elements are unquestionably important, and throughout my career I witnessed organizations invest enormous effort into developing strategies, building business cases, assembling talented teams, and acquiring the technologies they believed would secure their future.

Yet I also witnessed something that became impossible to ignore.

Organizations with brilliant strategies sometimes failed spectacularly.

Companies with exceptional people still struggled to achieve the value they expected.

Projects delivered on time and within budget occasionally produced disappointing business outcomes.

Acquisitions celebrated on closing day often failed to deliver the shareholder value that justified the investment.

The common denominator was rarely a lack of intelligence or effort.

It was execution.

Over the years, that realization fundamentally changed how I viewed leadership, transformation, and organizational success. I came to understand that execution is not simply the final phase of a project or the responsibility of a project manager. It is an enterprise capability that connects vision to reality, investment to outcomes, and strategy to measurable value.

That realization became the foundation for everything you have read in this book.

Although many of the examples have focused on mergers and acquisitions, the principles of enterprise value realization extend far beyond a single discipline. Every organization invests time, capital, technology, and human effort with the expectation of creating a better future. Whether that investment takes the form of an acquisition, a digital transformation, an ERP implementation, a capital project, an organizational redesign, or a strategic growth initiative, the challenge remains remarkably consistent.

How do we ensure the value we promised is the value we ultimately realize?

I believe that question deserves far more attention than it receives today.

For too long, organizations have measured success through activity rather than outcomes. We celebrate completed projects, signed agreements, deployed systems, and achieved milestones. While those accomplishments matter, they are not the destination. They are simply milestones along the journey toward something much more important: creating sustainable enterprise value.

True success is not measured by what an organization builds.

It is measured by what an organization becomes.

Organizations that consistently realize value share common characteristics. They establish clear objectives. They create alignment between strategy and execution. They make decisions quickly. They understand dependencies before they become obstacles. They measure progress continuously. They adapt without losing sight of their purpose. Most importantly, they recognize that execution is not an event—it is a culture.

That culture is not created by chance.

It is built intentionally.

It is reinforced through leadership.

It is strengthened through governance.

It is enabled by technology.

It is sustained through accountability.

And it is measured by the value it creates.

My hope is that this book encourages leaders to think differently about execution. I hope it challenges organizations to move beyond measuring schedules and budgets and begin measuring confidence, readiness, benefits, capability, and enterprise value. I hope it inspires executives to ask better questions, project leaders to think more strategically, and boards of directors to evaluate success not only by what has been delivered, but by the value that has been realized.

If these ideas lead to better decisions, stronger leadership, more successful transformations, or even one acquisition that achieves its full potential, then this book will have accomplished its purpose.

The journey toward enterprise value realization does not begin with a new methodology or a new technology platform.

It begins with a decision.

A decision to treat execution as a strategic capability.

A decision to lead with discipline.

A decision to measure what truly matters.

A decision to hold ourselves accountable for outcomes rather than activity.

Every organization has opportunities.

Every organization has ambitions.

Every organization has the potential to create extraordinary value.

The difference between those that succeed and those that fall short is rarely opportunity itself.

The difference is the ability to execute with clarity, discipline, and purpose.

As you leave these pages and return to your own organization, I encourage you to ask one simple question:

Are we managing work, or are we realizing value?

The answer to that question may shape every decision that follows.

Thank you for allowing me to share the lessons I have learned throughout my career. My sincere hope is that they help you build stronger organizations, lead more successful transformations, and create lasting value for your employees, your customers, your investors, and the communities you serve.

Because in the end, strategies inspire.

Investments enable.

Technology accelerates.

Leadership guides.

But only execution transforms vision into reality.

And that is why, above all else,

Execution determines value.

Appendix A - AVA Assess™ Readiness Checklist

Purpose

The AVA Assess™ Readiness Checklist is designed to help leaders evaluate whether their organization possesses the capacity, alignment, and capabilities necessary to successfully execute a transaction, transformation, integration, separation, or major strategic initiative.

This assessment is not intended to delay decisions.

It is intended to improve them.

Organizations that understand their readiness are better positioned to protect value, allocate resources, identify risks, and execute successfully.

Leadership Alignment
Strategic Alignment

☐ Executive leadership agrees on the strategic objectives.

☐ Success criteria have been clearly defined.

☐ Expected benefits have been documented.

☐ Major risks have been discussed.

☐ Leadership understands the value drivers.

☐ Executive sponsorship has been established.

Leadership Commitment

☐ Leaders have committed the necessary time.

☐ Leadership responsibilities are clearly defined.

☐ Decision authority is understood.

☐ Escalation paths have been established.

☐ Executive governance meetings are scheduled.

Assessment Score: ____ / 10

Organizational Capacity
Resource Availability

☐ Key resources have been identified.

☐ Functional leaders have committed resources.

☐ Subject matter experts are available.

☐ Backfill requirements have been identified.

☐ Critical roles have been assigned.

Competing Priorities

☐ Major competing initiatives have been identified.

☐ Resource conflicts have been evaluated.

☐ Leadership understands capacity limitations.

☐ Priority conflicts have been addressed.

☐ Additional support requirements have been identified.

Assessment Score: ____ / 10

Governance and Decision Making
Governance Structure

☐ Governance committees have been established.

☐ Roles and responsibilities are documented.

☐ Escalation procedures are defined.

☐ Reporting expectations are understood.

☐ Decision rights are documented.

Decision Readiness

☐ Executive decision makers are identified.

☐ Decision timelines are established.

☐ Approval processes are understood.

☐ Issue escalation procedures exist.

☐ Decision bottlenecks have been identified.

Assessment Score: ____ / 10

Technology Readiness
Systems and Applications

☐ Critical applications have been identified.

☐ Major dependencies have been documented.

☐ Technology risks have been assessed.

☐ Data considerations have been reviewed.

☐ Infrastructure impacts are understood.

Technology Resources

☐ Technology staffing requirements are known.

☐ Key technology resources are available.

☐ Cybersecurity considerations have been reviewed.

☐ Integration requirements have been identified.

☐ Technology governance exists.

Assessment Score: ____ / 10

Organizational Readiness
Change Readiness

☐ The organization understands the upcoming changes.

☐ Communication plans have been developed.

☐ Change impacts have been identified.

☐ Training requirements have been assessed.

☐ Adoption risks have been evaluated.

Cultural Alignment

☐ Leadership messages are aligned.

☐ Organizational resistance has been considered.

☐ Employee concerns have been identified.

☐ Stakeholder impacts have been evaluated.

☐ Change champions have been identified.

Assessment Score: ____ / 10

Value and Benefits
Benefit Definition

☐ Expected benefits have been documented.

☐ Value drivers have been identified.

☐ Benefit owners have been assigned.

☐ Measurement approaches have been established.

☐ Benefit timelines are understood.

Value Risks

☐ Major value risks have been identified.

☐ Assumptions have been documented.

☐ Leading indicators have been defined.

☐ Value leakage risks have been assessed.

☐ Benefit dependencies are understood.

Assessment Score: ____ / 10

Risk and Dependency Assessment
Risk Management

☐ Major risks have been identified.

☐ Risk ownership has been assigned.

☐ Mitigation actions have been defined.

☐ Escalation thresholds exist.

☐ Risk reviews have been scheduled.

Dependency Management

☐ Cross-functional dependencies have been identified.

☐ Critical path activities are understood.

☐ External dependencies have been assessed.

☐ Resource dependencies are visible.

☐ Technology dependencies have been reviewed.

Assessment Score: ____ / 10

AVA Assess™ Executive Summary

Category	Score
Leadership Alignment	____ / 10

Category	Score
Organizational Capacity	____ / 10
Governance & Decisions	____ / 10
Technology Readiness	____ / 10
Organizational Readiness	____ / 10
Value & Benefits	____ / 10
Risks & Dependencies	____ / 10

Total Score: ______ / 70

Readiness Interpretation
60–70 Points: High Readiness

The organization demonstrates strong readiness to execute. Risks exist but appear manageable. Leadership alignment, capacity, governance, and value management are generally well established.

45–59 Points: Moderate Readiness

Several areas require attention before execution accelerates. Leadership should review identified weaknesses and implement corrective actions.

30–44 Points: Elevated Risk

Significant readiness gaps exist. Capacity, governance, technology, or organizational issues may threaten value realization.

Below 30 Points: High Execution Risk

The organization may lack the necessary conditions to execute successfully. Immediate intervention and leadership attention are recommended.

Executive Reflection Questions

Before beginning execution, leadership should ask:

- Are we truly prepared to execute?
- Do we have sufficient organizational capacity?
- Are our leaders aligned?
- Do we understand our technology risks?
- Have we assigned ownership for benefits?
- What threatens value?
- What decisions must occur immediately?
- Where are we most vulnerable?

The purpose of AVA Assess™ is not to eliminate risk.

The purpose is to understand it.

Organizations cannot prepare for every challenge.

But organizations that understand themselves before execution begins are far more likely to realize the value they seek.

Because readiness does not guarantee success.

But a lack of readiness frequently guarantees difficulty.

Appendix B - 100-Day Integration Plan Template

Purpose

The first 100 days following transaction close represent one of the most important periods in enterprise value realization.

This period establishes:

- Leadership credibility.
- Organizational confidence.
- Decision-making processes.
- Governance structures.
- Technology direction.
- Benefit ownership.
- Execution momentum.

The objective of the first 100 days is not to complete the integration.

The objective is to establish the conditions necessary to realize value.

Executive Objectives

The first 100 days should accomplish five objectives:

1. Stabilize the business.
2. Establish governance.
3. Build organizational confidence.
4. Accelerate value realization.
5. Position the organization for long-term success.

Day 1 Priorities

Business Continuity

☐ Operations continue without disruption.

☐ Critical systems remain operational.

☐ Customer service continues.

☐ Financial processes function normally.

☐ Safety and compliance activities remain intact.

Leadership Communication

☐ Leadership communication issued.

☐ Employee messaging completed.

☐ Customer communications delivered.

☐ Key stakeholders informed.

☐ Immediate concerns addressed.

Organizational Stability

☐ Leadership teams confirmed.

☐ Escalation procedures activated.

☐ Critical roles identified.

☐ Immediate risks reviewed.

☐ Command center established if necessary.

Days 1–30: Stabilize and Assess Leadership Alignment

☐ Executive objectives confirmed.

☐ Success criteria established.

☐ Decision rights defined.

☐ Governance structure activated.

☐ Leadership cadence established.

Governance

☐ Steering committee established.

☐ Integration Management Office activated.

☐ Reporting structure implemented.

☐ Escalation procedures defined.

☐ Decision logs established.

Risk Management

☐ Top enterprise risks identified.

☐ Risk ownership assigned.

☐ Risk review process established.

☐ Issue escalation process activated.

☐ Dependency management process initiated.

AVA Assess™ Review

☐ Organizational capacity evaluated.

☐ Leadership alignment confirmed.

☐ Technology readiness assessed.

☐ Value risks identified.

☐ Readiness gaps documented.

Days 31–60: Execute and Accelerate Organizational Integration

☐ Organizational structures finalized.

☐ Functional leadership roles confirmed.

☐ Resource requirements validated.

☐ Critical vacancies identified.

☐ Workforce impacts communicated.

Technology Activities

☐ Technology roadmap approved.

☐ System dependencies identified.

☐ Cybersecurity risks assessed.

☐ Data requirements validated.

☐ Technology priorities established.

Value Realization

☐ Benefit owners assigned.

☐ Value drivers confirmed.

☐ Benefit measurement approach established.

☐ Leading indicators identified.

☐ Value risks reviewed.

Decision Velocity

☐ Decision backlog reviewed.

☐ Escalations addressed.

☐ Bottlenecks identified.

☐ Governance effectiveness evaluated.

☐ Leadership interventions completed.

Days 61–100: Sustain and Transition
Operational Stability

☐ Operating model functioning.

☐ Performance metrics established.

☐ Organizational responsibilities transferred.

☐ Business ownership confirmed.

☐ Support structures established.

Benefits Realization

☐ Initial benefits measured.

☐ Synergy progress evaluated.

☐ Value risks reassessed.

☐ Benefit forecasts updated.

☐ Leadership review completed.

Technology Stabilization

☐ Critical systems stabilized.

☐ Support responsibilities transferred.

☐ Outstanding risks documented.

☐ Operational ownership established.

☐ Future technology priorities identified.

Transition Readiness

☐ Temporary teams evaluated.

☐ Long-term ownership assigned.

☐ Remaining risks documented.

☐ Capability transfer completed.

☐ Sustainability plan established.

Executive Governance Cadence

Meeting	Frequency	Purpose
Executive Steering Committee	Biweekly	Decisions and value realization
IMO Leadership Meeting	Weekly	Execution management
Functional Leadership Review	Weekly	Cross-functional coordination
Risk Review	Weekly	Risk identification and mitigation
Value Assurance Review	Monthly	Protection of enterprise value
Benefits Review	Monthly	Benefits realization

First 100-Day Metrics
Leadership

- Executive participation rate
- Decision cycle time

- Escalation resolution time

Execution

- Milestone achievement
- Issue aging
- Risk trends

Technology

- System stability
- Critical incidents
- Technology readiness

Value

- Benefits achieved
- Synergy realization
- Value risks

Organization

- Employee retention
- Change adoption
- Resource capacity

Top 10 Executive Questions

1. Are operations stable?
2. Are our leaders aligned?
3. What threatens value?
4. Where are decisions delayed?
5. What risks are increasing?
6. Are resources sufficient?
7. Are benefits still achievable?
8. Is technology enabling execution?
9. Is the organization adapting?

10. Are we realizing value?

100-Day Executive Dashboard

Category	Status	Trend
Leadership Alignment	Green / Yellow / Red	↑ ↓ →
Organizational Capacity	Green / Yellow / Red	↑ ↓ →
Governance	Green / Yellow / Red	↑ ↓ →
Technology Readiness	Green / Yellow / Red	↑ ↓ →
Risk Exposure	Green / Yellow / Red	↑ ↓ →
Benefits Realization	Green / Yellow / Red	↑ ↓ →
Transition Readiness	Green / Yellow / Red	↑ ↓ →

AVA Value Assurance Review

At Day 30:

☐ Are value assumptions still valid?

☐ Have new risks emerged?

☐ Are leadership behaviors supporting execution?

☐ Is capacity sufficient?

☐ Are benefits protected?

At Day 60:

☐ Is execution progressing?

☐ Are decisions timely?

☐ Are dependencies managed?

☐ Is value leakage occurring?

☐ Are interventions required?

At Day 100:

☐ Is the organization stable?

☐ Have benefits begun to materialize?

☐ Can temporary structures transition?

☐ Is ownership established?

☐ Is value sustainable?

The AVA 100-Day Principle

Many organizations believe the first 100 days are about speed.

The first 100 days are actually about establishing momentum.

Leadership credibility.

Governance.

Accountability.

Decision making.

Technology stability.

Benefit ownership.

Execution discipline.

The organizations that realize value during the first 100 days are not necessarily those that move the fastest.

They are the organizations that establish the strongest foundation.

Because the first 100 days do not determine whether the work is completed.

They determine whether the value can ultimately be realized.

Appendix C - Executive Governance Cadence

Purpose

Successful organizations execute with rhythm.

Leadership teams meet consistently.

Decisions occur quickly.

Risks become visible.

Issues are resolved.

Benefits are reviewed.

Accountability is reinforced.

This operating rhythm creates what can be described as governance cadence.

Governance cadence is the structured sequence of leadership interactions that drive execution, accelerate decisions, and protect enterprise value.

The purpose of governance is not oversight.

The purpose of governance is results.

The Principles of Executive Governance

Effective governance should:

- Accelerate decision making.
- Increase leadership visibility.

- Reinforce accountability.
- Surface risks early.
- Resolve issues quickly.
- Protect enterprise value.
- Maintain organizational alignment.

Poor governance creates bureaucracy.

Effective governance creates execution.

The Executive Governance Model

The AVA Executive Governance Cadence consists of five levels:

1. Executive Steering Committee
2. Integration Management Office
3. Functional Leadership Teams
4. Risk and Value Reviews
5. Benefits Realization Reviews

Each level serves a different purpose.

Together they create the operating system of execution.

Executive Steering Committee
Purpose

Provide executive leadership, strategic direction, and major decision authority.

Participants

- Executive Sponsor
- Business Leadership
- Functional Executives
- Technology Leadership

- Finance Leadership
- Integration Leader

Frequency

Biweekly during critical phases.

Monthly during stabilization.

Typical Duration

60–90 minutes.

Primary Responsibilities

- Approve major decisions.
- Remove organizational barriers.
- Resolve escalated issues.
- Review value realization.
- Confirm strategic alignment.
- Reinforce priorities.

Key Questions

- Are we realizing value?
- What decisions require leadership?
- What risks threaten outcomes?
- Where should leadership intervene?

Integration Management Office Review Purpose

Coordinate enterprise execution.

Participants

- IMO Leader

- Workstream Leaders
- Program Leadership
- PMO Support

Frequency

Weekly.

Typical Duration

60 minutes.

Agenda

- Milestone review.
- Decision review.
- Risk review.
- Dependency review.
- Capacity review.
- Escalations.

Key Questions

- What changed this week?
- What decisions are needed?
- What risks are increasing?
- What issues require escalation?

Functional Leadership Reviews
Purpose

Align business functions.

Participants

- Functional Leaders
- Workstream Leads

- Subject Matter Experts

Frequency

Weekly.

Typical Duration

30–60 minutes.

Focus Areas

- Functional activities.
- Resource needs.
- Dependencies.
- Risks.
- Decisions.

Key Questions

- Are priorities aligned?
- Are resources sufficient?
- What support is required?

Risk Review Meeting
Purpose

Provide visibility into enterprise risks.

Participants

- Leadership Team
- Risk Owners
- IMO Leadership
- Technology Leadership

Frequency

Weekly or biweekly.

Typical Duration

30 minutes.

Discussion Areas

- New risks.
- Risk trends.
- Mitigation plans.
- Escalations.
- Emerging threats.

Executive Questions

- What threatens value?
- Which risks are increasing?
- What actions are required?

AVA Assure™ Value Review
Purpose

Protect enterprise value.

Participants

- Executive Sponsor
- Value Owners
- IMO Leadership
- Finance Leadership
- Functional Leaders

Frequency

Monthly.

Typical Duration

60 minutes.

Review Topics

- Benefits realization.
- Value leakage indicators.
- Leadership alignment.
- Decision effectiveness.
- Execution health.

Key Questions

- Is value protected?
- Are benefits still achievable?
- What threatens realization?

Benefits Realization Review

Purpose

Measure outcomes.

Participants

- Business Leadership
- Finance
- Benefit Owners
- Executive Sponsors

Frequency

Monthly or quarterly.

Discussion Areas

- Benefit performance.

- Synergy realization.
- Financial outcomes.
- Operational improvements.
- Future opportunities.

Executive Questions

- Are benefits materializing?
- Who owns the outcomes?
- What actions are necessary?

Governance Meeting Rules

Successful governance meetings follow several principles.

Decision-Oriented

Meetings exist to make decisions.

Time Disciplined

Meetings begin and end on time.

Action Focused

Discussions lead to actions.

Escalation Driven

Barriers receive attention.

Value Focused

Outcomes receive priority.

Leadership Led

Executives actively participate.

Sample Weekly Governance Cadence

Day	Meeting	Purpose
Monday	Functional Reviews	Team alignment
Tuesday	Risk Review	Risk visibility
Wednesday	IMO Review	Enterprise coordination
Thursday	Executive Steering Committee	Decisions
Friday	Leadership Communications	Alignment

Monthly Governance Cadence
Week 1

Executive Steering Committee

Week 2

Value Assurance Review

Week 3

Benefits Realization Review

Week 4

Leadership Strategy Session

This rhythm creates consistency.

Consistency creates predictability.

Predictability improves execution.

Executive Dashboard

The executive governance dashboard should include:

Leadership

- Executive participation.
- Decision cycle time.

Execution

- Milestone confidence.
- Issue aging.

Risk

- High-risk items.
- Escalation trends.

Technology

- System readiness.
- Critical incidents.

Value

- Benefits achieved.
- Value leakage indicators.

Organization

- Capacity.
- Adoption.
- Change readiness.

Decision Escalation Model

Level 1

Functional leadership.

Level 2

IMO leadership.

Level 3

Executive Steering Committee.

Level 4

Executive Sponsor.

Escalation should accelerate decisions.

Not delay them.

Governance Health Indicators

Organizations should monitor:

- Decision cycle times.
- Escalation aging.
- Leadership attendance.
- Issue resolution rates.
- Risk closure rates.
- Benefit realization trends.
- Value leakage indicators.

Governance itself can be measured.

Healthy governance improves execution.

Executive Reflection Questions

- Are decisions occurring quickly enough?
- Are risks visible?
- Are leaders engaged?
- Are issues being resolved?
- Is accountability clear?
- Are benefits protected?
- Is value being realized?

The AVA Governance Principle

Many organizations measure governance by the number of meetings held.

The more important measures are:

- Decisions made.
- Risks resolved.
- Barriers removed.
- Benefits realized.
- Value protected.

Governance is not an administrative process.

It is the operating rhythm of enterprise execution.

Because organizations execute at the speed of decisions.

Decisions occur through governance.

And governance ultimately determines whether value is realized.

Appendix D - Value Leakage Early Warning Indicators

Purpose

Value leakage rarely occurs as a single event.

Organizations seldom wake up one morning and discover that value has disappeared overnight.

Instead, value is typically lost gradually.

Delayed decisions.

Leadership distractions.

Technology problems.

Resource shortages.

Unresolved risks.

Benefit erosion.

These conditions often appear weeks or months before financial performance deteriorates.

The purpose of this appendix is to help leaders identify these early warning indicators before value is lost.

The objective is not prediction.

The objective is visibility.

Organizations that recognize these signals early can intervene, protect value, and improve outcomes.

The AVA Value Leakage Principle

Expected Value

– Value Leakage

= Realized Value

Organizations frequently focus on increasing expected value.

However, improving realized value often depends more upon reducing value leakage.

Early identification creates opportunities for intervention.

Intervention protects value.

Leadership Indicators
Executive Participation Declines
Warning Signs

- Steering committee attendance declines.
- Executive delegates attend meetings.
- Decisions remain unresolved.
- Leadership attention shifts elsewhere.

Potential Impact

- Delayed decisions.
- Reduced accountability.
- Organizational uncertainty.

Recommended Actions

- Re-engage leadership.
- Clarify priorities.

- Escalate critical decisions.

Conflicting Leadership Messages
Warning Signs

- Different priorities communicated.
- Leaders disagree publicly.
- Teams receive conflicting guidance.

Potential Impact

- Confusion.
- Delayed execution.
- Reduced confidence.

Recommended Actions

- Conduct alignment sessions.
- Clarify objectives.
- Reconfirm priorities.

Decision Indicators
Increasing Decision Cycle Time
Warning Signs

- Decisions require multiple meetings.
- Approval processes lengthen.
- Escalations increase.

Potential Impact

- Schedule delays.
- Dependency impacts.
- Resource inefficiencies.

Recommended Actions

- Clarify decision rights.
- Reduce approval layers.
- Escalate unresolved issues.

Growing Decision Backlog
Warning Signs

- Open decisions increase.
- Teams wait for approvals.
- Critical activities pause.

Potential Impact

- Execution slows.
- Risks increase.
- Value realization delays.

Recommended Actions

- Prioritize decisions.
- Increase executive involvement.
- Accelerate governance.

Capacity Indicators
Resource Overload
Warning Signs

- Key resources support multiple initiatives.
- Overtime increases.
- Work backlogs develop.

Potential Impact

- Burnout.
- Delays.
- Quality issues.

Recommended Actions

- Add resources.
- Reprioritize work.
- Provide leadership support.

Critical Resource Dependence
Warning Signs

- One individual owns multiple activities.
- Subject matter experts become bottlenecks.
- Decisions depend upon limited resources.

Potential Impact

- Delays.
- Knowledge risks.
- Increased vulnerability.

Recommended Actions

- Develop backups.
- Expand expertise.
- Reduce dependencies.

Governance Indicators
Escalations Increase
Warning Signs

- More issues require leadership attention.
- Functional leaders cannot resolve conflicts.
- Escalation meetings increase.

Potential Impact

- Governance strain.

- Leadership overload.
- Execution delays.

Recommended Actions

- Improve decision authority.
- Strengthen accountability.
- Clarify ownership.

Meeting Activity Increases
Warning Signs

- Additional meetings appear.
- Status reporting expands.
- Decisions remain unresolved.

Potential Impact

- Reduced productivity.
- Organizational fatigue.
- Slower execution.

Recommended Actions

- Focus meetings on decisions.
- Eliminate unnecessary reporting.
- Simplify governance.

Technology Indicators
Technology Milestones Slip
Warning Signs

- System dates move.
- Testing delays occur.
- Integration activities slip.

Potential Impact

- Operational risk.
- Schedule delays.
- Increased costs.

Recommended Actions

- Reassess priorities.
- Add resources.
- Increase executive attention.

Data Quality Problems Increase
Warning Signs

- Data defects increase.
- Reporting discrepancies emerge.
- Reconciliation efforts expand.

Potential Impact

- Decision quality declines.
- Operational disruptions.
- Delayed benefits.

Recommended Actions

- Improve data governance.
- Increase validation efforts.
- Assign ownership.

Organizational Indicators
Employee Fatigue
Warning Signs

- Engagement declines.

- Frustration increases.
- Turnover rises.

Potential Impact

- Reduced productivity.
- Loss of knowledge.
- Resistance to change.

Recommended Actions

- Reduce workload.
- Improve communication.
- Increase leadership visibility.

Resistance Increases
Warning Signs

- Adoption slows.
- Participation declines.
- Informal opposition grows.

Potential Impact

- Delayed implementation.
- Reduced benefits.
- Cultural challenges.

Recommended Actions

- Improve communications.
- Increase engagement.
- Address concerns directly.

Benefits Indicators
Benefits Ownership Is Unclear

Warning Signs

- No owner exists.
- Metrics are undefined.
- Accountability is absent.

Potential Impact

- Unrealized benefits.
- Value erosion.
- Poor visibility.

Recommended Actions

- Assign ownership.
- Establish measurements.
- Review regularly.

Benefit Forecasts Decline
Warning Signs

- Savings estimates decrease.
- Timelines extend.
- Expectations change.

Potential Impact

- Reduced value.
- Leadership concerns.
- Business case erosion.

Recommended Actions

- Review assumptions.
- Identify corrective actions.
- Reassess priorities.

Transition Indicators
Temporary Solutions Become Permanent
Warning Signs

- Manual processes continue.
- Interim systems remain.
- Workarounds increase.

Potential Impact

- Increased costs.
- Reduced efficiency.
- Sustainability risks.

Recommended Actions

- Establish deadlines.
- Assign ownership.
- Accelerate transition.

Knowledge Transfer Is Incomplete
Warning Signs

- Key individuals retain critical knowledge.
- Documentation is limited.
- Support capabilities are weak.

Potential Impact

- Operational risk.
- Dependency issues.
- Reduced sustainability.

Recommended Actions

- Increase training.

- Document processes.
- Develop capabilities.

AVA Value Leakage Dashboard

Indicator	Green	Yellow	Red
Leadership Engagement	High	Declining	Low
Decision Velocity	Fast	Slowing	Delayed
Resource Capacity	Adequate	Constrained	Overloaded
Governance Health	Effective	Inconsistent	Ineffective
Technology Readiness	Stable	Concerns	High Risk
Organizational Adoption	Strong	Mixed	Weak
Benefits Realization	On Track	Delayed	At Risk
Transition Readiness	Ready	Concerns	Unprepared

Executive Questions

Leaders should regularly ask:

- What has changed?
- What concerns us most?
- What decisions are delayed?
- Where are resources constrained?
- What threatens value?
- Which benefits are at risk?
- What assumptions have changed?
- Where should leadership intervene?

AVA Assure™ Review Questions
Leadership

Are leaders engaged?

Governance

Are decisions occurring?

Capacity

Can the organization absorb the work?

Technology

Are systems enabling value?

Benefits

Are outcomes materializing?

Sustainability

Will value survive the transition?

The Value Leakage Principle

Organizations often believe value is lost because of major failures.

In reality, value is usually lost through a series of small events:

One delayed decision.

One unresolved risk.

One overloaded team.

One missed dependency.

One benefit that nobody owns.

One assumption that changes.

These events accumulate.

Eventually, the value expected at the beginning becomes difficult to achieve.

The organizations that consistently realize value are not those that avoid every problem.

They are the organizations that recognize problems early.

Because value rarely disappears without warning.

Organizations are almost always told.

The challenge is recognizing the signals before value is lost.

Appendix E - Benefits Realization Dashboard

Purpose

Organizations frequently measure activities.

Milestones completed.

Tasks finished.

Budgets spent.

Schedules achieved.

These measurements are important.

However, they do not answer the most important question.

Are we realizing the expected value?

The purpose of the Benefits Realization Dashboard is to provide leadership with visibility into value realization throughout the lifecycle of a transaction, integration, separation, transformation, or strategic initiative.

The dashboard shifts the conversation from:

- What work has been completed?

To:

- What value has been realized?

Executive Summary Dashboard

Category	Status	Trend	Owner
Financial Benefits	Green / Yellow / Red	↑ ↓ →	CFO
Operational Benefits	Green / Yellow / Red	↑ ↓ →	COO
Technology Benefits	Green / Yellow / Red	↑ ↓ →	CIO
Organizational Benefits	Green / Yellow / Red	↑ ↓ →	Business Leader
Strategic Benefits	Green / Yellow / Red	↑ ↓ →	Executive Sponsor
Overall Value Realization	Green / Yellow / Red	↑ ↓ →	Executive Team

Financial Benefits Dashboard

Benefit	Target	Actual	Variance	Trend	Owner
Cost Synergies	$_____	$_____	$_____	↑ ↓ →	
Procurement Savings	$_____	$_____	$_____	↑ ↓ →	
Operating Costs	$_____	$_____	$_____	↑ ↓ →	
Revenue Growth	$_____	$_____	$_____	↑ ↓ →	
EBITDA Improvement	$_____	$_____	$_____	↑ ↓ →	

Executive Questions

- Are financial benefits appearing as expected?
- Have assumptions changed?
- Are corrective actions necessary?

Operational Benefits Dashboard

Benefit	Target	Actual	Status
Process Efficiency			
Productivity			
Cycle Time Reduction			
Service Performance			
Operational Stability			

Executive Questions

- Are operations improving?
- Are efficiencies materializing?
- Are performance levels sustainable?

Technology Benefits Dashboard

Benefit	Target	Actual	Status
System Stability			
Application Consolidation			
Technology Costs			
Data Quality			
User Adoption			

Executive Questions

- Is technology enabling value?
- Are systems supporting the business?
- Are technology risks increasing?

Organizational Benefits Dashboard

Benefit	Target	Actual	Status
Leadership Alignment			
Employee Engagement			
Decision Velocity			
Organizational Capacity			
Change Adoption			

Executive Questions

- Is the organization adapting?
- Are leaders aligned?
- Is the workforce supporting the change?

Strategic Benefits Dashboard

Benefit	Target	Actual	Status
Market Expansion			
Competitive Position			
New Capabilities			
Customer Experience			
Growth Opportunities			

Executive Questions

- Are strategic objectives being achieved?
- Is the organization more capable?
- Are long-term benefits emerging?

Benefit Ownership Register

Benefit	Owner	Target Date	Status

Every significant benefit should have:

- A clear owner.
- A target date.
- A measurement method.
- Executive visibility.

Benefits without ownership frequently remain unrealized.

Benefit Status Definitions

Green

Benefit is on track.

Performance meets expectations.

No immediate intervention required.

Yellow

Potential concerns exist.

Performance requires attention.

Leadership review recommended.

Red

Benefit is at risk.

Corrective actions are required.

Executive intervention necessary.

Value Realization Trend Analysis

Quarter	Expected Value	Realized Value	Variance
Q1			
Q2			
Q3			
Q4			

Trend analysis provides visibility into:

- Improving performance.
- Emerging risks.
- Benefit erosion.
- Value leakage.

Value Leakage Indicators

Monitor:

☐ Benefit delays.

☐ Declining forecasts.

☐ Ownership changes.

☐ Decision delays.

☐ Technology issues.

☐ Resource constraints.

☐ Organizational resistance.

☐ Increased risks.

Early visibility protects value.

AVA Assure™ Benefit Review

The monthly value assurance review should evaluate:

Leadership

- Are leaders engaged?

Benefits

- Are outcomes appearing?

Risks

- What threatens realization?

Ownership

- Who owns each benefit?

Actions

- What intervention is required?

Benefits Realization Scorecard

Category	Score (1–5)
Financial Benefits	
Operational Benefits	
Technology Benefits	
Organizational Benefits	
Strategic Benefits	
Benefit Ownership	
Measurement Discipline	
Executive Visibility	

Scoring

36–40: Excellent Value Realization

28–35: Strong Performance

20–27: Moderate Risk

Below 20: Significant Value Risk

Executive Questions

Leadership should regularly ask:

- What value have we realized?
- What value remains unrealized?
- What benefits are at risk?
- Who owns the outcomes?
- What assumptions have changed?
- What actions are required?

The AVA Benefits Principle

Projects deliver outputs.

Organizations realize outcomes.

The purpose of execution is not:

- Completing tasks.
- Finishing milestones.
- Closing projects.

The purpose of execution is realizing value.

If value is important enough to justify the investment, it is important enough to measure.

Organizations that continuously measure benefits often realize more value.

Organizations that stop measuring frequently discover that benefits disappear.

Because benefits realization does not happen automatically.

It requires visibility.

Ownership.

Accountability.

Leadership.

And a relentless focus on outcomes.

That is the purpose of the Benefits Realization Dashboard.

To ensure that expected value becomes realized value.

Appendix F - Technology Risk Assessment Matrix

Purpose

Technology influences virtually every aspect of modern transactions, integrations, separations, and transformations.

Applications support operations.

Data drives decisions.

Systems enable processes.

Infrastructure supports business continuity.

Cybersecurity protects the enterprise.

Technology failures frequently create:

- Operational disruption.
- Delayed benefits.
- Increased costs.
- Extended timelines.
- Reduced confidence.
- Value leakage.

The purpose of this Technology Risk Assessment Matrix is to help leaders identify, assess, and manage technology risks that threaten enterprise value.

The objective is not to eliminate all technology risk.

The objective is to understand, prioritize, and manage the risks that matter most.

The AVA Tech™ Technology Principle

Technology does not create value by itself.

Technology enables:

- Execution.
- Operations.
- Decisions.
- Performance.
- Benefits realization.

Technology risk therefore becomes value risk.

Technology Risk Categories

The AVA Tech™ Technology Risk Assessment evaluates six major areas:

1. Applications
2. Data
3. Infrastructure
4. Cybersecurity
5. Resources and Capacity
6. Operational Sustainability

Risk Assessment Method

Each risk should be evaluated using:

Score	Probability	Impact
1	Low	Minimal
2	Moderate	Limited
3	Significant	Material

Score	Probability	Impact
4	High	Major
5	Critical	Severe

Risk Score:

Probability × Impact

Score	Risk Level
1–5	Low
6–10	Moderate
11–15	High
16–25	Critical

Application Risk Assessment

Risk Area	Probability	Impact	Score
Legacy Applications			
Unsupported Systems			
Application Dependencies			
Integration Complexity			
Third-Party Software			
Licensing Risks			

Executive Questions

- Which applications are business critical?
- What systems create dependencies?
- Which systems represent operational risk?

Data Risk Assessment

Risk Area	Probability	Impact	Score
Data Quality			
Data Ownership			
Data Migration			
Reporting Integrity			

Risk Area	Probability	Impact	Score
Master Data Issues			
Regulatory Data Requirements			

Executive Questions

- Is the data reliable?
- Who owns the data?
- Can the organization trust its information?

Infrastructure Risk Assessment

Risk Area	Probability	Impact	Score
Network Stability			
Cloud Dependencies			
Disaster Recovery			
Business Continuity			
Capacity Limitations			
Infrastructure Obsolescence			

Executive Questions

- Can infrastructure support future operations?
- Are resilience plans adequate?
- Where are single points of failure?

Cybersecurity Risk Assessment

Risk Area	Probability	Impact	Score
Vulnerabilities			
Identity Management			
Access Controls			
Third-Party Risk			
Regulatory Compliance			
Incident Response			

Executive Questions

- Has security been evaluated?
- Are access controls sufficient?
- Could cyber risk threaten value?

Technology Capacity Assessment

Risk Area	Probability	Impact	Score
Resource Availability			
SME Capacity			
Skill Gaps			
Vendor Dependency			
Competing Priorities			
Leadership Capacity			

Executive Questions

- Does the organization have sufficient technology resources?
- Where are bottlenecks?
- What expertise is missing?

Operational Sustainability Assessment

Risk Area	Probability	Impact	Score
Support Readiness			
Knowledge Transfer			
Operational Ownership			
Documentation Quality			
Training Effectiveness			
Transition Readiness			

Executive Questions

- Can the organization support the environment?
- Is ownership established?
- Will value survive the transition?

Technology Dependency Matrix

Dependency Owner Risk Level Mitigation

Critical dependencies should receive executive visibility.

Technology Readiness Scorecard

Category	Score (1–5)
Applications	
Data	
Infrastructure	
Cybersecurity	
Capacity	
Sustainability	

Total Score: _____ / 30

Technology Risk Interpretation

25–30: Low Risk

Technology environment supports execution.

19–24: Moderate Risk

Some areas require attention.

13–18: Elevated Risk

Several risks may threaten value realization.

Below 13: High Technology Risk

Executive intervention recommended.

Technology Early Warning Indicators

Leaders should monitor:

☐ Increasing incident volume.

☐ Delayed technology milestones.

☐ Data quality problems.

☐ Resource overload.

☐ Rising cybersecurity concerns.

☐ Growing technical debt.

☐ System instability.

☐ Extended workarounds.

These indicators frequently appear before major problems emerge.

AVA Tech™™ Executive Dashboard

Category	Status	Trend
Applications	Green / Yellow / Red	↑ ↓ →
Data	Green / Yellow / Red	↑ ↓ →
Infrastructure	Green / Yellow / Red	↑ ↓ →
Cybersecurity	Green / Yellow / Red	↑ ↓ →
Capacity	Green / Yellow / Red	↑ ↓ →
Sustainability	Green / Yellow / Red	↑ ↓ →

Technology Risk Heat Map

Impact	Probability	Risk Level
Low	Low	Green
Moderate	Moderate	Yellow
High	High	Red

Impact	Probability	Risk Level
Critical	Critical	Red

The purpose of the heat map is to prioritize leadership attention.

Not all risks deserve equal focus.

AVA Assure™ Technology Review

The monthly value assurance review should ask:

- Are technology risks increasing?
- Are systems enabling execution?
- Is data supporting decisions?
- Are resources sufficient?
- Can operations be sustained?
- What threatens value?

Technology risk should always be evaluated through the lens of value realization.

Executive Questions

- Which technology risks threaten value?
- Where are our greatest dependencies?
- Do we have sufficient technology capacity?
- Are systems enabling the business?
- Can the future organization support these solutions?
- What decisions are required?

The AVA Tech™ Technology Principle

Technology organizations often measure:

- Servers.

- Applications.
- Incidents.
- Projects.

The enterprise measures:

- Performance.
- Benefits.
- Outcomes.
- Value.

Technology risk matters because value matters.

The organizations that consistently realize value understand that technology is not simply an IT concern.

Technology influences:

- Execution.
- Decisions.
- Operations.
- Benefits.
- Sustainability.

Technology does not merely support the business.

Technology increasingly enables the business.

And the risks that threaten technology often threaten value itself.

Appendix G - AVA Enterprise Value Realization Governance Model

Successful organizations recognize that enterprise value realization requires more than project management. It requires leadership alignment, clear accountability, effective governance, disciplined decision-making, and continuous oversight across the entire organization.

Traditional program management offices often focus primarily on schedules, actions, and status reporting. While these activities remain important, modern value realization requires a broader governance model that aligns leadership, operations, technology, execution, and long-term sustainability.

The AVA Enterprise Value Realization Governance Model provides a structure that supports the five AVA pillars while enabling AVA Intelligence™ and AVA Assure™ to operate across the entire enterprise.

Executive Steering Committee

Primary Responsibilities

- Strategic direction.
- Enterprise priorities.
- Capital allocation.
- Value realization oversight.
- Executive decision making.
- Risk acceptance.
- Organizational alignment.

Typical Members

- Chief Executive Officer
- Chief Financial Officer
- Business Leadership
- Executive Sponsors
- Functional Executives

- Transformation Sponsors

Meeting Cadence

Monthly or as required for major decisions.

Enterprise Value Realization Office (EVRO)

The Enterprise Value Realization Office serves as the central coordinating organization responsible for integrating the five AVA pillars.

Responsibilities

- Enterprise governance.
- Program coordination.
- Cross-functional integration.
- Value realization management.
- Executive reporting.
- Dependency management.
- Benefits tracking.

The EVRO may function as an Integration Management Office, Transformation Office, Program Management Office, or Value Realization Office depending upon the organization.

AVA ASSESS™ GOVERNANCE

Responsibilities

- Readiness assessments.
- Risk evaluations.
- Opportunity analysis.
- Capacity assessments.
- Due diligence support.
- Complexity evaluation.
- Value driver identification.

Leadership Roles

- Business Sponsors
- Strategy Leaders
- Risk Management
- Functional Leadership

AVA EXECUTE™ GOVERNANCE

Responsibilities

- Program management.
- Execution planning.
- Governance administration.
- Issue management.
- Dependency coordination.
- Benefits realization.
- Delivery oversight.

Leadership Roles

- Program Director
- Integration Leader
- Transformation Leader
- Workstream Leaders

AVA LEAD™ GOVERNANCE

Responsibilities

- Executive alignment.
- Stakeholder management.
- Organizational readiness.
- Change leadership.
- Communication.
- Decision facilitation.
- Talent engagement.

Leadership Roles

- Executive Sponsors
- Change Leaders
- HR Leadership
- Communications Teams

AVA TECH™™ GOVERNANCE

Responsibilities

- Technology strategy.

- Architecture decisions.
- Data management.
- Cybersecurity.
- Application integration.
- Infrastructure readiness.
- Technology risk management.

Leadership Roles

- Chief Information Officer
- Technology Leaders
- Cybersecurity Teams
- Enterprise Architects

AVA EXIT™ GOVERNANCE

Responsibilities

- Transition planning.
- TSA management.
- Operational readiness.
- Sustainability planning.
- Ownership transfer.
- Dependency retirement.
- Long-term support models.

Leadership Roles

- Business Owners
- Transition Managers
- Operations Leadership
- Support Organizations

AVA INTELLIGENCE™

AVA Intelligence™ supports every governance level by providing:

- Predictive analytics.
- Trend analysis.
- Early warning indicators.
- Risk forecasting.
- Executive insights.
- Scenario analysis.

- Performance analytics.

Questions AVA Intelligence™ helps answer:

- Where is value at risk?
- What decisions are slowing progress?
- Which risks are increasing?
- Where are dependencies emerging?
- Which benefits are at risk?

AVA ASSURE™

AVA Assure™ provides independent oversight across the entire system.

Assurance Activities

- Value assurance reviews.
- Health assessments.
- Benefits realization reviews.
- Governance reviews.
- Risk assessments.
- Executive reporting.
- Independent validation.

Recommended review points:

□ Opportunity assessment.
□ Planning complete.
□ Day One readiness.
□ Mid-execution review.
□ Technology readiness.
□ Transition readiness.
□ Benefits realization.

Decision Escalation Framework

Decision Type	Owner	Escalation
Operational	Workstream Leaders	Program Leadership
Functional	Functional Leaders	Executive Sponsors
Technology	Technology Leadership	Executive Steering Committee
Organizational	Business Leadership	Executive Steering Committee
Strategic	Executive Sponsors	Board or Executive Leadership

Recommended Meeting Cadence

Meeting	Frequency
Executive Steering Committee	Monthly
EVRO Leadership	Weekly
Pillar Leadership Team	Weekly
Workstream Reviews	Weekly
Risk Review	Biweekly
Value Assurance Review	Quarterly
Benefits Realization Review	Quarterly
Executive Value Review	Semiannual

Example Organizational Model

Executive Steering Committee

Enterprise Value Realization Office

Assess Execute Lead Tech Exit

AVA Intelligence™

AVA Assure™

Final Thought

Governance exists to create clarity, accelerate decisions, align leadership, and protect enterprise value.
Organizations that govern only schedules often miss emerging risks.
Organizations that govern value create sustainable results.

The future of enterprise execution will require governance systems that integrate readiness, execution, leadership, technology, transition, intelligence, and assurance into a single enterprise model.

That is the purpose of the AVA Enterprise Value Realization Governance Model.

I think this new Appendix G is substantially stronger than the original IMO appendix because it becomes the operational blueprint for the entire AVA Enterprise Value Realization System and ties directly to the five pillars, AVA Intelligence™, and AVA Assure™.

Appendix H - Enterprise Value Realization Early Warning Indicators

Enterprise value is rarely lost in a single event. In most organizations, value erodes gradually through a series of small signals, unresolved issues, delayed decisions, and declining organizational alignment. These warning indicators often appear months before measurable impacts become visible.

The purpose of this appendix is to help executives, integration leaders, program managers, and transformation teams identify potential threats to value realization before those threats become significant business problems.

The AVA Enterprise Value Realization System recognizes that risks can emerge across any of the five pillars. Effective organizations monitor these indicators continuously and respond before value begins to leak from the system.

AVA ASSESS™ WARNING INDICATORS

Readiness Risks

□ Undefined value drivers.
□ Incomplete business case.
□ Unclear success criteria.
□ Inadequate due diligence.
□ Missing risk assessments.
□ Unrealistic assumptions.
□ Limited resource capacity.
□ Undefined ownership.
□ Poor organizational readiness.
□ Incomplete stakeholder analysis.

Early Symptoms

- Different leaders describe success differently.
- Risks continue to emerge after execution begins.
- Resource requirements exceed available capacity.

- Teams lack clarity regarding objectives.

AVA EXECUTE™ WARNING INDICATORS

Execution Risks

□ Milestones repeatedly missed.
□ Decisions delayed.
□ Escalations unresolved.
□ Program reporting inconsistent.
□ Growing issue backlog.
□ Increasing dependency conflicts.
□ Benefits not being tracked.
□ Accountability unclear.
□ Governance meetings ineffective.
□ Execution teams overloaded.

Early Symptoms

- Teams spend more time reporting than executing.
- Actions remain open for multiple reporting cycles.
- Program schedules continually shift.
- Leaders lose confidence in status reporting.

AVA LEAD™ WARNING INDICATORS

Leadership Risks

□ Executive engagement declining.
□ Conflicting leadership messages.
□ Poor stakeholder communication.
□ Organizational resistance increasing.
□ Decision ownership unclear.
□ Leadership turnover.
□ Low team morale.
□ Change fatigue.
□ Escalating conflict.
□ Accountability avoidance.

Early Symptoms

- Employees receive conflicting direction.
- Decisions repeatedly return for reconsideration.

- Stakeholder support weakens.
- Teams lose confidence in leadership.

AVA TECH™™ WARNING INDICATORS

Technology Risks

□ Data migration delays.
□ Cybersecurity concerns unresolved.
□ Application dependencies unidentified.
□ Infrastructure readiness concerns.
□ Integration defects increasing.
□ Technology TSA dependencies unresolved.
□ ERP schedules slipping.
□ Testing defects rising.
□ System performance issues.
□ Technology resources constrained.

Early Symptoms

- Technology becomes a schedule driver.
- Business processes depend on temporary workarounds.
- Manual activities increase.
- Operational risks begin to rise.

AVA EXIT™ WARNING INDICATORS

Transition Risks

□ TSA exit dates slipping.
□ Operational ownership unclear.
□ Knowledge transfer incomplete.
□ Remaining dependencies unresolved.
□ Support models undefined.
□ Long-term accountability unclear.
□ Benefits sustainability uncertain.
□ Transition activities delayed.
□ Operational stabilization incomplete.
□ Exit criteria undefined.

Early Symptoms

- Temporary solutions become permanent.

- Organizations continue to rely on legacy support.
- Ownership remains ambiguous.
- Expected benefits begin to decline.

AVA INTELLIGENCE™ INDICATORS

AVA Intelligence™ seeks to identify patterns before problems become visible.

Indicators include:

□ Declining decision velocity.
□ Increasing issue aging.
□ Resource overload trends.
□ Escalation frequency increasing.
□ Dependency concentrations.
□ Risk clustering.
□ Benefits forecast deterioration.
□ Organizational sentiment changes.
□ Executive engagement declines.
□ Schedule confidence reduction.

Predictive indicators often provide the earliest evidence that value realization may be at risk.

AVA ASSURE™ REVIEW TRIGGERS

Value assurance reviews should be considered when:

□ Major milestones are missed.
□ Benefit forecasts decline.
□ Leadership changes occur.
□ Scope significantly changes.
□ Technology risks increase.
□ Decision cycles slow.
□ Organizational resistance grows.
□ Transition activities slip.
□ Resource constraints increase.
□ Executive confidence declines.

Periodic assurance reviews provide independent validation that value remains achievable.

EXECUTIVE VALUE DASHBOARD

Indicator	Green	Yellow	Red
Schedule Performance	On Track	Minor Delays	Significant Delays
Decision Velocity	Timely	Slowing	Stalled
Leadership Alignment	Strong	Mixed	Fragmented
Resource Capacity	Adequate	Constrained	Critical
Technology Readiness	Ready	At Risk	Delayed
Transition Readiness	Stable	Concern	High Risk
Benefits Realization	On Target	Trending Down	Off Target
Stakeholder Support	High	Declining	Low
Value Leakage Risk	Low	Moderate	High

Executives should routinely monitor:

Final Thought

Value rarely disappears suddenly.

Organizations often receive numerous warning signals long before value is lost. The challenge is not the absence of information. The challenge is recognizing those signals early enough to act.

Organizations that continuously assess readiness, execute with discipline, lead through change, enable technology, prepare for transition, apply intelligence, and provide assurance place themselves in the strongest position to realize enterprise value.

The goal is not simply to identify problems.

The goal is to protect value before it is lost.

I actually think this new Appendix H may become one of the strongest practical tools in the entire book because it directly ties the five pillars, AVA Intelligence™, and AVA Assure™ together into something executives can immediately use.

www.ingramcontent.com/pod-product-compliance
Lightning Source LLC
LaVergne TN
LVHW100256210926
848480LV00003B/937

* 9 7 9 8 9 9 6 6 0 7 8 0 8 *